All About
HIGH-FREQUENCY
TRADING

MICHAEL DURBIN

 Mc Graw Hill

New York Chicago San Francisco Lisbon London Madrid Mexico City
Milan New Delhi San Juan Seoul Singapore Sydney Toronto

1 2 3 4 5 6 7 8 9 10 11 12 13 14 15   WFR/WFR   1 9 8 7 6 5 4 3 2 1 0

ISBN   978-0-07-174344-0
MHID   0-07-174344-8

This publication is designed to provide accurate and authoritative information in regard to the subject matter covered. It is sold with the understanding that neither the author nor the publisher is engaged in rendering legal, accounting, securities trading, or other professional services. If legal advice or other expert assistance is required, the services of a competent professional person should be sought.
> —From a Declaration of Principles Jointly Adopted by a Committee of the American Bar Association and a Committee of Publishers and Associations

McGraw-Hill books are available at special quantity discounts to use as premiums and sales promotions or for use in corporate training programs. To contact a representative, please e-mail us at bulksales@mcgraw-hill.com.

This book is printed on acid-free paper.

CONTENTS

Customer: How much are these?
Merchant: A buck fifty.
Customer: I'll take some.
Merchant: They're a buck fifty-one.
Customer: Um, you said a buck fifty.
Merchant: That was before I knew you wanted some.
Customer: You can't do that.
Merchant: It's my shop.
Customer: But I need to buy a hundred!
Merchant: A hundred? Then it's a buck fifty-two.
Customer: You're ripping me off.
Merchant: Supply and demand, pal. You want 'em or not?

What is high-frequency trading? Great question! And it's about time for an answer, because everyone seems to be talking about it—and forming strong opinions about it—and when that happens, it's usually a good thing to know just what *it* is. Does high-frequency trading relate only to stock trading? Or does it include automated trading of stock derivatives such as options? Does it encompass any type of automated trading, where computers make the decisions humans once did? Or does it pertain only to the dubious practices of the ~~sharks~~ sophisticated trading firms who, like the merchant above, move markets in their favor just because they can get away with it? Well, since nobody can quite answer these questions, let's just make our own definition and get on with it.

In general, *high-frequency trading* (HFT) refers to the buying or selling of securities wherein success depends on how quickly you act, where a delay of a few thousandths of a second, or milliseconds,[1] can mean the difference between profit and loss. HFT happens not only in the stock markets but in the markets for stock options and futures as well. Naturally, not every reason for trading requires speedy execution. Certainly not, say, buying stock because you think the company will do well over the coming years or cashing out your 401(k) to buy the Harley you've had your eye on since you were sixteen. But plenty of trading strategies do indeed depend on how quickly you can spot a profitable trading opportunity in the market—and how quickly you respond with a trade order to seize that opportunity before somebody else does. We'll describe a number of such strategies later on.

The high-frequency trader evolved from the ranks of the traditional market-maker, or *specialist*, whose primary source of profit was the spread between the prices at which he bought and sold. Unlike the traditional market-maker, however, and owing to developments like decimalization[2] and advances in technology, the high-frequency trader must settle for much narrower spreads—razor-thin margins of a penny or less. As such, high-frequency traders operate in massive scales. Indeed, the larger high-frequency trading firms now glide through the markets scooping up vast mouthfuls of trades like a whale does krill.

Signs of the likely effects of high-frequency trading, and the growth of the number of firms practicing it, are not hard to find. Figure 1 shows the Security and Exchange Commission's (SEC) calculation of the nearly threefold increase in daily

---

[1] Increasingly, and perhaps by the time you read this book, microseconds—or millionths of a second—also matter. And it's only a matter of time before we're talking about nanoseconds, or billionths of a second.

[2] *Decimalization* refers to the shift, in the early 2000s, from trading stocks in fractions of dollars to doing so in pennies, dramatically reducing the potential spread between the prices at which one can buy and sell a stock.

FIGURE 1

NYSE Trading Statistics

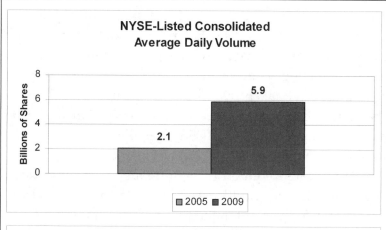

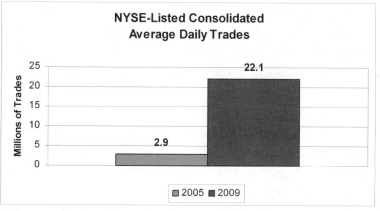

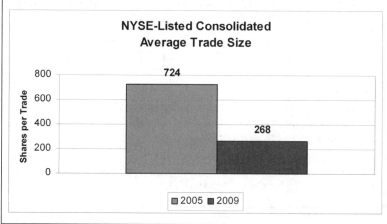

trading volume[3] of New York Stock Exchange (NYSE)–listed
stocks between 2005 and 2009, alongside the nearly *eight-fold* increase over the same period in the number of trades
executed each day, which together imply the shrinkage of the
average trade size, as also shown.[4] Such data is reasonably
consistent with what you would expect with more and more
firms competing to make markets.[5] The real indicator that
computers have taken over, however, is in Figure 2, which
shows the reduction in average trade execution time from
more than ten seconds in 2005 to less than one second four
years later. Humans are fast, but not that fast.

The speeds required of high-frequency trading exceed
anything a human could ever match. As such, HFT is, by
necessity, a form of automated trading. It's trading wherein
computers make the real-time tactical decisions that used
to be made by humans back in the olden days. It's rather
like an autopilot in this respect. On most modern aircraft, a
computer makes the moment-to-moment decisions that keep
the plane aloft and on track—flap positions, air speed, and
so on. That computer was designed and programmed based
on decades of manual flying experience. The strategies and
procedures humans developed for flying a plane have been
expressed in the electronics and software of a machine. There
is still a human pilot in the cockpit, however. She keeps an
eye on the autopilot, turning it on when safe to do so, setting
its controls correctly, and taking over when necessary.

High-frequency trading represents the same sort of evolution. And *evolution* is just the right word because, just like

---

[3] Volume gives the number of shares traded in a given period.

[4] U.S. Securities and Exchange Commission, "Concept Release on Equity
Market Structure," 1/14/2010 [Release 34-61358; File S7-02-10].

[5] It's also consistent with the concern, which we'll get to later on, that
much of this new trading volume is among high-frequency trading firms
themselves, trading for the sake of trading.

FIGURE 2

NYSE Average Speed of Execution*

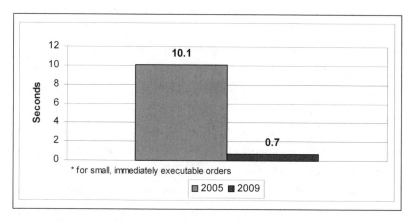

the autopilot, high-frequency trading wasn't invented over-night. HFT represents the current evolution of the technologi-cal element of the securities markets. That evolution has been going on for decades and will continue indefinitely. Speeds we consider fast today are likely to be considered pathetically slow before we know it.

While quite a lot of trading qualifies as high-frequency trading in this general sense, there is a very specific type of HFT getting loads of attention these days, not much of it positive, centering as it does on concerns over safety and fair-ness. The controversial style of high-frequency trading—the type of HFT this book is mainly about—uses amazingly fast computation and networking capabilities to perform a type of trading strategy known rather ignobly as *scalping*. Like a ticket scalper at a ballpark, the securities scalper attempts to buy at one price and quickly sell at a higher price, or vice versa, pocketing the so-called bid-ask spread between the two. One of those prices typically belongs to a mispriced security, for example, a stock priced lower or higher than it should be. The chief work of the high-frequency trader, then, is to find these opportunities and exploit them before anyone else does. (More later on how this is done.)

This book, a flyover of the high-frequency trading landscape, is written and organized for the reader with little or no prior knowledge of, well, anything to do with trading. The first thing we'll do is lay a foundation for understanding high-frequency trading by reviewing the various types of equity securities and the crucial relationships among them. We'll also take some time to understand what actually happens at the exchange and get ourselves good and comfortable with the order book, where trading actually happens. After a review of fundamental trading concepts, and a segregation of traders into four archetypes we'll call *investor, marketmaker, arbitrageur*, and *predictor*, we'll dive promptly into their respective strategies and see where the high-frequency trader fits into the picture. As already noted, there is no shortage of concern these days about the perceived risks of highfrequency trading, so we'll dutifully summarize those and attempt to give equal time to its supposed benefits as well as discuss the more dubious purported practices of some highfrequency trading firms.

The information and assertions in this book are based on my own direct experience, as well as that of a number of traders, exchange officials, and others in the industry who were kind enough to talk with me. To the best of my knowledge, nothing revealed in this book could reasonably be considered proprietary to any individual firm. While highfrequency traders are well known for zealously guarding their trade secrets, there is still plenty of common knowledge to be had about high-frequency trading, certainly enough for you to get your bearings if you are new to this corner of the financial universe. Oh, and before I forget, let me say with no equivocation that as of the publication of this book, there is no way of telling which of the trading strategies discussed herein would be considered legal and which would not. The propriety (whether by legal or ethical standards) of HFT is itself currently one of the subjects of a rather heated debate at the SEC, on Wall Street, and on exchanges around the world, so I do not offer up these words as anything even remotely resembling investment advice. Not to put too fine a point on it, but please don't attempt to employ any trading methodologies discussed in this book just because you read about them here.

You may have heard how much money can supposedly be earned by high-frequency trading. As such, I know what at least some of you might be thinking: "Can I do this at home?" Would that you could. Sure, you can pick up a gaming computer at Best Buy with processing power comparable to what the HFT firms have inside their servers. But you can also buy the same football they use in the Super Bowl at Sports Authority and the same Stratocaster you might see in the hands of Eric Clapton at Guitar Center. As you'll hopefully begin to appreciate after reading these pages, fast computers, like pigskins and guitars, are not the only gear one needs to play in this game.

ACKNOWLEDGMENTS

For all manner of assistance in preparation of this book, I owe thanks to Matthew Goldstein of Reuters; to Bill Brodsky and Ed Tilly of the Chicago Board Options Exchange; to the most unique Julie Langsdorf; to Alfred Berkeley and Ken Burke of Pipeline Trading Systems; to Tom Boggs, Richard Co, Brett Vietmeier, and Phillip Hatzopoulos of the CME Group; to Bernard Donefer of Baruch College CUNY; to traders Ray Boesen, Vincent Florack, and Phil Scherrer; to Bryan Harkins of Direct Edge; to Jonah Crane; to my family's favorite science guy, Jim Mueller; to others who provided invaluable background information (you know who you are); to my editor Morgan Ertel of McGraw-Hill for her patience and persistence; to Julia Anderson Bauer, Marisa L'Heureux, and the rest of the McGraw-Hill production team for making my work look much more polished than I ever could; and to my dear Marlow and Greta, for tolerating and supporting yet another of Dad's writing projects.

CHAPTER 1

Busted

I always wondered when word would get out. I got my own look in 2003. That's when I went to work for the Citadel Investment Group, Ken Griffin's stealthy Chicago hedge fund, to help them build a high-frequency trading system for the U.S. equity options market. There was only one fully automated options exchange in the United States at that time, the International Securities Exchange (ISE) in New York. Before the ISE opened for business in 2000, no options exchange would allow market-makers (a type of trader we'll learn about presently) to submit their all-important quotations—bids to buy and offers to sell—electronically. For the most part, those were still communicated verbally by human traders with loud voices and sharp elbows, standing all day in open outcry trading pits wearing sensible shoes. ISE founders David Krell and Gary Katz knew it was time to change that, and the success of their enterprise proved to any remaining doubters how absolutely right they were. The ISE was the quintessential game changer. Their explosive success forced the traditional, floor-based options exchanges to make their own plans for electronic quoting. And Ken Griffin wanted Citadel to be all over it.

I had been managing financial systems development for several years by this time, mostly for the pricing of derivative securities. The Citadel system, though, would not only calculate hundreds of thousands of option prices simultaneously—an impressive feat in its own right—but also inject streams of bids and offers into the markets at literally superhuman speed. The custom-built quoting engines would tirelessly inject many millions of quotes into the markets every day, each of them a binding commitment to buy or sell a listed option contract at some specified price, each one the result of a software program running on a computer. And while the quoters were busy doing that, "electronic eyes" would scan everyone else's quotations and orders—hundreds of millions per day—all in real time. It would be like standing at the end of an open fire hose and examining each drop of water before it hit the ground. When the electronic eye (or EE) found someone offering to buy an option for more than it was worth, or to sell it for less, it would immediately submit an order to take the other side of the trade for a tiny profit.

It was a dazzling sight, watching these machines pick the markets clean of its inefficiencies. I would have loved to talk about it back then, to tell friends and family what was going on in the gleaming glass tower at the intersection of Dearborn and Adams. But the confidentiality agreements one has to sign for employers like Citadel are very, very effective. In this business, everyone knows that loose lips get pink slips. So like everyone else, I kept my mouth shut and talked only with my small group of colleagues on the 37th floor.[1]

---

[1] Even within the sanctum sanctorum at Citadel, information was purely need-to-know. I once asked a quantitative analyst about one of the factors that went into the all-important volatility model. "What does 'v' mean?" "It means 'v,'" she replied. "Ahh. What about 'h'?" "It means 'h.'" This little badinage went on for quite a few more letters of the alphabet.

By the time I left Citadel in 2005, their options market-making system—the work of a team not much larger than the Chicago Cubs' starting lineup—was responsible for more than 10 percent of all options trading in the United States, or more than a million contracts a day. Within three years, its market share had reportedly grown to a commanding 30 percent. The U.S. options market had become dominated by the extraordinary machines of just a handful of secretive firms like Citadel. Still, nobody on the outside seemed to have a clue—or a care—that trading was no longer done by traders.

That all changed in 2009. As people licked their wounds in the aftermath of the 2008 market meltdown, wondering where all the money went, word got out that something like $20 billion of it went to these folks known as high-frequency traders. The term was well known inside firms like Citadel but not so much outside. Now, it was bad enough that *anyone* made out like bandits in the horrible year that was 2008, but a far more frightening contemplation caused more than a few people to go grab a pitchfork from the shed: Was high-frequency trading (HFT) somehow culpable? Did it cause the mother of all crashes or accelerate it once it began? After all, the 1987 market crash was widely attributed to automated trading, then known as program trading. Did the computers do it again?

Word went around that 50 percent of all stock trading—maybe 60 percent or even 70 percent—was attributable to HFT computers trading with each other, supposedly just to collect tiny kickbacks, known as rebates, from the exchange. The HFT firms weren't even holding on to their stock. Once bought, they'd immediately turn around and sell it, sometimes buying and selling the same stock hundreds or thousands of times a day. What was up with that? All this trading at ungodly speeds, it was said, was creating massive price volatility that otherwise wouldn't exist. Could this be good?

Nerves were not settled when a former Goldman Sachs employee was arrested for allegedly stealing proprietary computer code for high-frequency trading, with the bank asserting ominously, "There is a danger that somebody who (knows) how to use this program could use it to manipulate markets in unfair ways."[2] Computer code to manipulate markets? What the heck was going on here?

Anyone following the HFT stories in 2009 learned a handful of new terms from the modern trading lexicon— none of them particularly comforting. The HFT firms were supposedly using something called "flash orders" to get advance looks at customer trade orders before the rest of the market, then using those peeks to make their own trades at a profit. Wasn't that front-running and wasn't it illegal? The flash order robbers supposedly had only 30 milliseconds to do their dirty work, but this was plenty of time because they "colocated" their computer servers in the same data centers as the exchange computers, at great expense. This also let them get their own orders in before any investor possibly could. Uneven playing field, anybody?

Unsatisfied with flash order thievery, the HFT smarties supposedly submitted something called *immediate-or-cancel* (IOC) orders with no intention of trading, but only to force investors to reveal the true prices at which they were willing to trade, information the HFT guys would use to move market prices against the investor. Whoa. Were the HFT firms even qualified to be so close to the exchange and trade at lightning speeds? Nobody could say, because it was nearly impossible to know even the identities of high-frequency traders. They didn't need to make the infrastructure investments themselves. They could use *direct market access* (DMA)

---

[2] "Goldman May Lose Millions From Ex-Worker's Code Theft," Bloomberg, July 7, 2009.

or *naked access*, using their broker's exchange connection to get in anonymously, then perform their lightning-fast derring-do as if wearing a mask.[3]

"Dude," you could almost hear people asking, fatigued and more than a little ticked off, "What happened to our stock market?" Was it no longer what it used to be, a place to simply invest in companies with the idea of holding on to that stock for a while? Were we all foolishly naive to still think like that? Maybe we had all been reduced to easy marks for sharpies with fast computers and math skills far better than our own, like dummies on the boardwalk, sized up and taken by the hucksters. Do the markets still work? Or have they been hijacked by cutthroat information technology and runaway greed?

It can sure seem that way.

The year 2008 was indeed the year of wonders for high-frequency traders, especially options traders, and this struck plenty of folks as somehow wrong. A headhunter told me that his client, a high-frequency options market-making firm, had made over $800 million in 2008. Another well-known firm was said to have cleared $1.3 billion of net profit—and that was just trading options. Who knows what the stock HFT desk pulled in.

Having worked in this business and performed mind-numbing P&L[4] calculations myself, I found those rumored numbers entirely plausible. Three billion option contracts were traded in 2008[5] with a net profit to the market-maker

---

[3] SEC Chairman Mary Schapiro likens the practice of DMA to lending the car keys to your unregistered Ferrari to someone who may not even be licensed to drive.

[4] Profit and loss.

[5] optionsclearing.com/webapps/historical-volume-query.

of, let's say, $2.00 each.[6] That's $6 billion in profits across the entire market. Even if my estimate is high and the marketwide profit was more like $5 or even $4 billion, with so few market-makers having forks in that pie, it's entirely plausible that some of the slices were around $1 billion. Now, just because some people made out like kings in 2008 when most people suffered, however, does not mean all those gains were ill-gotten. When technology revolutionizes an industry, be it personal computing or automobile manufacturing or oil refining, it's not unheard-of for a small number of pioneers (Gates, Ford, Rockefeller) to make bazillions from their investments.

There's more mileage to be had from the automobile analogy, this time relating to safety. When horseless buggies first hit the streets in the early twentieth century, top speeds were on the order of 10 or 15 miles per hour, and there weren't all that many of these novelties on the road. As technology, demand, and free-market enterprise found their confluence, however, those top speeds climbed steadily and the roads started filling. Cars crashed, people died, and the lethality of these contraptions became frightfully obvious. Government and industry began addressing safety in the design and regulation of automobiles. Speed limits were posted, seat belts were invented, laws were written, and cops started writing tickets. It's not unreasonable to say that high-frequency trading requires that same sort of rethinking to

---

[6] This assumes an average trade edge of $0.03 (for example, a market-maker sells an option with a theoretical value of $5.00 for $5.03). The market-maker loses, say, one-third of this to the cost of hedging (maintaining a delta-neutral offsetting stock position, imperfections in volatility estimations, and so on). Most contracts are for 100 shares of the underlying security, so a quoted price is multiplied by 100 to arrive at an actual trade price (the market-maker receives $503.00 for the option listed at 5.03, or a trade profit of $3.00, which erodes to $2.00).

keep people safe in light of the new capabilities brought on by technology.

And there is yet one more obvious parallel between the automotive revolution and HFT. Some folks in the early years of the automobile saw cars not as conveniences but as tools to help commit crime. Would John Dillinger have fared so well were his getaway vehicle a trolley? Bank robbers used cars to get away with crimes they might not have otherwise. In turn, the cops themselves were equipped with better and better cars and laws were expanded and revised accordingly. Can people use the tools of high-frequency trading to get away with things they might not have, say, ten years ago? It's not inconceivable. Is it time to reconsider regulations and law enforcement in the securities markets? Probably.

It must be said that pulling off the high-frequency part of high-frequency trading is no stroll through the mall. It's exceedingly difficult setting up an HFT system that actually works, and there is no one thing to be done, no single task to master, any more than there is only one thing to ensure the successful construction of an ocean liner. High-frequency traders leave no stone unturned in pursuit of their wispy profits, starting with the hiring of just the right number of rock stars from the fields of trading, mathematics, and software system development. They write their own software rather than license packaged products from third parties, investing the time and money required for a system catered to their exact needs, one they can fix and modify on their own schedule. Oh, and for the building and maintaining of these systematic goliaths, they spend sums of money that would make even Warren Buffett raise his eyebrows.

HFT firms apply softare engineering practices that facilitate the development of software designed for change—because it must change continuously to keep up with the equally well-heeled and motivated Joneses—and they write exquisitely efficient code. Their systems are perfect examples of so-called distributed, real-time systems, borrowing patterns from the field of complex event processing, with thousands of individual programs running on just the right number of computers in just the right number of data centers. They buck the decades-long trend of packing more and more processing onto a computer's CPU (central processing unit), favoring the seemingly backward approach of delegating some computing tasks to specialized hardware. They even take over the massively parallel processing capability of graphical processing units—game cards, in essence—for financial computations.

An HFT firm would not dream of receiving market data—the crucial flow of "ticks"—or submitting trade orders by way of third parties and their latency-consuming connections. They insist on direct connections to the exchange for these purposes. Wherever they can, they forego the use of the industry standard FIX[7] protocol for communicating with the exchange, favoring the writing of software that talks directly to the native application programming interfaces, or APIs, of each exchange. They also know where the exchanges house their computers, or matching engines, and they lease space in the very same data centers to colocate their own servers, thus getting their work done just a few millionths of a second sooner than the next guy.

Exhausting? Expensive? You betcha. But with the prospect of rolling a billion simoleons a year off of one these money-making machines, it's no wonder more than one firm is willing to pay whatever it takes to have one.

---

[7] Financial Industry eXchange, an industry-standard protocol for electronic exchange of securities transactions. FIX is a wonderful thing in that it greatly simplifies things like trade order submissions, but some believe it adds a teensy tiny bit of time to the order-entry process.

CHAPTER 2

Trading 101

First things first: Before we address high-frequency trading, let's review a few things about plain old trading. Once we orient ourselves with respect to the equity-related securities traded on U.S. markets and the essence of what happens at a securities exchange—who does what and why, and some of the natural dynamics among various parties—we'll be in a better position to appreciate what happens when we step on the gas.

EQUITY SECURITIES

Many discussions of high-frequency trading pertain to listed cash equity securities, or stocks. But HFT also takes place in two securities closely related to stocks: equity options (stock options) and equity index futures. The U.S. markets for stocks, options, and futures are so deeply interconnected they act as one giant market in equity-based securities, and high-frequency trading is practiced extensively across that "supermarket." Indeed, more than being something that just happens to be practiced in each of those markets, it is arguably the very reason those markets are connected as tightly as they are.

In this book, we'll focus primarily on HFT in the stock markets, but we will also delve into options and futures HFT should you want to expand your view a bit, although that's certainly not necessary for a basic understanding of HFT. Moreover, and as we'll see later on, some of the strategies employed in the stock market are driven by what goes on in the futures and options markets, giving yet another reason you may want to be at least familiar with what goes on there. HFT is certainly not confined to the U.S. equity supermarket. It's becoming more and more prevalent in markets outside the United States and in nonequity markets such as those for commodities, interest rates, and currencies (aka, *foreign exchange* or FX). Although we won't discuss those directly in this book, many of the concepts we discuss pertain to those markets as well.

Stocks

A stock, of course, represents a sliver of ownership of a corporation. On a typical day, roughly 9 billion shares of stock are traded across the U.S. markets.[1] These stocks include not only the 5,000 or so listed equity securities issued by individual companies—Google (symbol GOOG), Alcoa (AA), Motorola (MOT), and so on—but also *exchange-traded funds*, or ETFs, which trade very much like traditional stock but whose value is based on an index. These have become extremely popular in recent years with some ETFs trading as heavily as the most actively traded stocks.

ETFs are sometimes known as *index tracking stocks*. For example, the value of the ETF known as the Spider (symbol SPDR) is by definition equal to approximately one-tenth that

---

[1] Average from 10/19/2009 through 11/13/2009 per market volume data provided at batstrading.com.

of the S&P 500 stock index.[2] Another extremely popular ETF tracks the NASDAQ-100 index (QQQQ, also known as "the Qs"). ETFs are listed right alongside single-name stocks and even pay cumulative dividends from the underlying stocks. There are dozens of traditional ETFs available, although a very small number tend to dominate the market. There are also new breeds of so-called leveraged ETFs whose daily returns are amplified by some factor (two or three, typically) versus a traditional ETF.

Options

Equity options are a type of derivative security that give their buyers the right to buy (in the case of *call* options) or sell (*put* options) an underlying stock or ETF at a specified strike price in a specified time frame, in return for payment of a premium. A popular variation of these is the index option, whose under-lier is not an individual stock or ETF but an index (you can think of it as a basket of stocks), such as the S&P 500. For a given stock or index, there may be hundreds of listed option contracts, each with a different strike price, expiration date, and type (call versus put). As a result, there are actually more listed option contracts than there are stocks—far more.

This fact is indeed one reason why HFT is well suited for options trading; there are simply so many contracts to keep track of, a computer can manage them much more effectively than can a human trader. The other reason options and HFT go together so well is the relationship between a stock price and a corresponding option price (or index level, in the case of index options). The price of an option depends on several

---

[2] By definition, it is exactly one-tenth, but there is often a divergence by a few pennies due to things like cost differences in trading Spiders versus the underlying index.

factors, but the most obvious of these is the current price of the underlying stock. When a stock price moves, the value of an option on it changes simultaneously; the price of an option is said to be derived (hence the term *derivative*) from the price of the stock. Only computers can recalculate option prices quickly enough for option prices to keep up with stock prices. (Sometimes even computers don't keep up. Later, we'll see how a lag in the process presents a nice opportunity known as arbitrage.)

Equity and equity index options have become extraordinarily popular securities over the past several years, with daily trading volumes in 2009 hovering around 14 million contracts.[3] Most contracts grant trading rights to 100 shares of the underlying stock. As such, options on roughly 1.4 billion shares of stock trade each day.

Futures

Equity index futures are another type of derivative security that allow you to effectively buy or sell the basket of stocks underlying an index, on a specified date in the future at a specified delivery price. As with index options, you don't actually buy or sell the basket (they are *cash-settled* contracts) but you gain or lose money as if you could and you realize those gains or losses daily. As such, to take a position in one of these futures is very much to make a bet on the market.

One of the most popular of these is the E-mini S&P 500 futures contract (ES) traded at the Chicago Mercantile Exchange (CME). Say it's late January and you purchase one ES for delivery in March with a price of $1,100. You have essentially committed yourself to buy a basket of 50 of each

---

[3] The Options Clearing Corporation maintains a fantastic website (options clearing.com) where it's as easy as pie to see what trades where in the U.S. options market.

of the 500 stocks comprising the S&P 500 index for a purchase price of $55,000.[4] You pay nothing for the contract itself.[5] The delivery price is set—based primarily on the current index level, interest rates, time to delivery, and expected dividends of the stocks—such that the contract has no value. That delivery price changes continuously throughout the trading day, and the value of your ES position changes with it. If the index rises, your position gains value; likewise, when the index falls, your position loses value.

Say the index is at $1,200 come the contract delivery date in March. The cost of the stock basket underlying your ES contract is now $60,000, or $5,000 more than you committed to pay. Assuming you held the contract through delivery, you gained roughly $5,000. (You actually gain slightly less because value changes in futures contracts are settled daily. As such, in this example, you would have received at least some of your gain prior to delivery date, with those payments effectively discounted according to prevailing interest rates.)

The ES might sound much like the option contract, but there is an important difference between options and futures. Had you committed to sell at that price (i.e., taken not a long but a short position in the ES futures contract), then you would have likewise lost roughly $5,000. Unlike options, futures bestow on their holders the obligation to a future purchase or sale of the underlier trade at a predetermined price, no matter the going or spot price come the delivery date. Remember, too, that futures contracts have no fundamental value at their outset, whereas option contracts always have value. An option's price can be thought of as an insurance premium for protection against loss.

---

[4] The notional value of one ES contract is $50 times the S&P 500 index level.

[5] You do pay brokerage and other transaction fees, but the contract itself has no fundamental value.

You can no doubt intuit why the markets for stocks, options, and futures are so tightly linked. Just think about any one of the 500 stocks that make up the S&P 500 stock index. A change in the perceived value of the issuing company clearly—and very directly—affects the price at which you can buy or sell that stock. But it also can have an effect on the price of outstanding option contracts on that stock. And as a component of the S&P 500 index, its value definitely influences the index level, which in turn affects the contract price of the index futures. Stock, options, and futures prices are thus inherently bound together, and only computers can do the math fast enough to keep these markets in sync.

THE EXCHANGE

The traditional venue for the trading of equity securities is the exchange. This is the physical place, the meeting ground if you will, where buyers and sellers of so-called listed securities come to find each other. An alternative to the exchange-based market, one we won't consider here, is the *over the counter* (OTC) market where parties find each other and negotiate privately.[6,7]

Another mechanism for trading is known as *internalization*, wherein a customer's broker can itself take the other side

---

[6] Aside from private counterparty identification and negotiation, the OTC market is also distinguished from the exchange markets by less product standardization and lack of centralized trade clearing as well as its comparatively loose means of ensuring counterparty performance (i.e., doing what you promise to do when you make a trade), features exchange traders take for granted. It's more than an academic distinction. In 2008, the OTC market for mortgage-based derivatives, such as credit default swaps, contributed to the worst U.S. economic disaster since the Great Depression due in very large part to widespread counterparty default.

[7] The NASDAQ once was, and occasionally still is, referred to as an OTC market. But that classification, really anachronistic nowadays, is not what we mean here by OTC. For our purposes, the NASDAQ is very much an exchange.

of a customer order, provided certain conditions are met, such as the setting of the price at no worse than what the customer could obtain on the open market (more on this when we get to national best bid and offer—NBBO—later in this chapter). At the securities exchange, however, one publicly announces bids to buy some number of securities at some price and/or offers to sell at some price. This goes on until one party's bid matches another party's offer, at which time—voilà!—a trade is made. The precise matching rules vary somewhat from exchange to exchange, but the basic idea is very much the same.

Now the typical exchange sells not just one security but gobs of them. For example, at the NYSE, one can trade any of 3,000 or so different stocks. At the Chicago Board Options Exchange (CBOE), there are nearly *300,000* contracts to choose from. As a public meeting place for the trading of a rich variety of goods, an exchange is not unlike a bazaar of ancient times. The word *bazaar*, in fact, is said to be derived from the Persian *baha-char*, or "place of prices." Sounds just like an exchange.

Stock, Options, and Futures Exchanges

Table 2.1 lists the current "big four" U.S. markets for stocks (in alphabetical order) where the great majority of stock trading takes place, along with the geographical location of their *matching engine*. This is the physical computer server (or, more likely, the bank of computer servers) that literally matches prospective buyers with prospective sellers the instant they agree on a price and quantity.

The matching engine replaces the open outcry trading pit as the singular physical place where trading actually happens; we'll see how it happens when we turn presently to the order book. It only stands to reason that the more proximate one is to the matching engine, the faster you can get information into and out of the exchange. As such, the aggressive

TABLE 2.1

U.S. Stock Exchanges

Exchange	Matching Engine
BATS	Weehawken, NJ
Direct Edge	Jersey City, NJ (2010: Secaucus, NJ)
NASDAQ	Carteret, NJ
NYSE	Weehawken, NJ (2010: Mahwah, NJ)

HFT firm will try to place their own computers as close as possible to the exchange-matching engines—ideally in the very same data center—in a practice that has come to be known as *colocating* with the exchange.

The parallel between colocation and a common tactic applied daily on traditional, floor-based trading is obvious. For example, human traders in the SPX[8] pit at the Chicago Board Options Exchange still, to this day, jockey for positions next to the most active brokers. The trader literally rubbing elbows and occasionally stepping on the toes of a broker receiving a big order by headset is more likely to get a piece of it than the trader five bodies away, moshed so hard he may be lucky to just raise an arm or get out for a pee break. The benefit of optimal colocation in the trading pit is well known, so it's no wonder HFT firms apply the same thinking when deciding where to place their servers. And do you notice how all four major stock exchanges have their matching engines in New Jersey? The Garden State can rightly add Colocation Capital of the World to its many noteworthy accolades.[9]

---

[8] The SPX is a highly liquid index option whose underlying value is based on the current level of the S&P 500 stock index.

[9] Along with being the home of Bruce Springsteen, the state most likely to be slandered by comedians, and one of only two states where you still can't pump your own gas, the other being Oregon, which to my knowledge has not even one colocation facility.

TABLE 2.2

U.S. Options Exchanges

Exchange	Matching Engine
BATS Options	Weehawken, NJ
Boston Options Exchange (BOX)	Newark, NJ (2010: Secaucus, NJ)
Chicago Board Options Exchange (CBOE)	Chicago, IL
CBOE C2 (2010)	Secaucus, NJ
Chicago Mercantile Exchange (CME)	Chicago, IL
Intercontinental Exchange (ICE)	Chicago, IL
International Securities Exchange (ISE)	Jersey City (2010: Secaucus, NJ)
NASDAQ Options Market (NOM)	Carteret, NJ
NASDAQ PHLX	Carteret, NJ
NYSE AMEX	Weehawken, NJ (2010: Mahwah, NJ)
NYSE Arca	Weehawken, NJ (2010: Mahwah, NJ)

Table 2.2 is a breakdown of the current and planned U.S. options exchanges. Note that the CME and ICE trade futures options, as opposed to "cash" options on stocks and ETFs and their indices traded elsewhere. An index futures option allows you, for a price, to gain the right but not the obligation to take a long or short position in a futures contract. These deliver, then, in neither cash nor stock, but in a futures contract on the stock index.

And rounding out the mix, Table 2.3 shows the current U.S. exchanges where most equity index futures trade. Please note that you can also trade futures options at these exchanges.[10]

---

[10] Depending on your reasons for perusing these pages, you may like to note that for reasons utterly lacking in either rhyme or reason, U.S. futures exchanges are regulated not by the SEC, as are stock and option markets, but by the Commodity Futures Trading Commission.

TABLE 2.3

U.S. Equity Index Futures Exchanges

Exchange	Matching Engine
Chicago Mercantile Exchange (CME)	Chicago, IL
Intercontinental Exchange (ICE)	Chicago, IL

Alternative Trading Systems

Time was you could trade a popular U.S. stock anywhere you wanted so long as it was the NYSE.[11] Or at least it seemed that way. The venerable Big Board began losing its near monopoly in the waning years of the twentieth century, and for the first decade of the twenty-first saw that trend only accelerate. Even as recently as 2005, the NYSE could boast that nearly 80 percent of the trading of NYSE-listed stocks still actually traded there, but that ample slice of the pie would shrivel to just 25 percent by 2009.[12] Where did the trading go? Much of it went to a slew of venues the SEC refers to as *alternative trading systems* (ATSs). This is a catch-all term that encompasses any place that matches prospective stock buyers and sellers that isn't, well, an exchange (options and futures, for the most part, still trade on a traditional exchange).

The term *ATS* used to refer to trading venues that matched buyers and sellers electronically, as opposed to a physical trading floor at a traditional exchange, but since all exchanges now match electronically that distinction is anachronistic to say the least. An ECN, or *electronic crossing*

---

[11] Concept shamelessly borrowed, of course, from Henry Ford.

[12] U.S. Securities and Exchange Commission, "Concept Release on Equity Market Structure," 1/14/2010 [Release No. 34-61358; File No. S7-02-10]. "NYSE executed approximately 79.1% of the consolidated share volume in its listed stocks in January 2005, compared to 25.1% in October 2009."

network, is a very popular ATS, which acts very much like an exchange but publishes its quotes not directly but by way of NASDAQ. A *dark pool* is an ATS that does not disseminate, or display, its quotes at all.[13] And a venue may start out as an ATS (e.g., BATS) and change to an exchange later on.

It's all very confusing, with distinctions having to do with things like where trades "print" (get published) and "clear" (become finalized) and whatnot, fortunately of no huge concern to us for the moment. Unless specifically noted otherwise, all references to trading in this book shall be to that which takes place on an exchange. Most trading still does take place at an exchange.[14] And the important thing for our purposes, the thing at the heart of any of these venues and that which makes them essentially more alike than different, is the all-important order book.

THE ORDER BOOK

At a bazaar in old Persia, parties might congregate at one stall or another depending on what goods they wished to trade: rugs over there, sheep right here, camel blankets down by the olive tree. At each stall, prospective buyers would negotiate and haggle with prospective sellers until some agreement was met. Then, the two parties in agreement might step away to actually carry out their trade—or clear it, if you will—by exchanging the goods for coins or onions or whatever. At a modern securities exchange, where buyers and sellers are matched predominantly by electronic means, the haggling is done at a place known as the *order book*. Every exchange

---

[13] Later we'll learn about reserve orders, which an exchange considers for purposes of matching but does not display. A dark pool is not terribly unlike an exchange where all orders and quotations are treated this way.

[14] The newest of these being the former ECN Direct Edge, granted exchange status by the SEC in March 2010.

or ATS uses order books, and they all work pretty much the same way. Like rods in the core of a nuclear reactor, the order books are where all the action is.

For all intents and purposes, there is one book per security at an exchange. For a given security, say stock in Acme Explosives, Inc. (symbol AEX), the order book might look something like this:

---

500 | 1.00 × 1.10 | 600

The prices in the middle are the quoted *bid* and *ask* price, respectively (the ask price is also known as the *offer* price). The bid is the price at which some party—or some group of parties—is willing to buy. The ask/offer price is the price at which someone is willing to sell. If you want to buy, then, you consider the offer price. To sell, look at the bid. The numbers on the outside are the respective quantities available at those prices. Want to buy these securities? Someone will sell you up to 600 of them for a dollar and ten cents. Want to sell? Someone is willing to buy as many as 500 for a buck. Note, by the way, the identity of quoters is not revealed. Only the exchange knows who is bidding and offering.

These four numbers, visible at all times to anyone with an interest in trading on the exchange, are known collectively as the *BBO* for "best bid and offer" and at first glance might seem rather uninteresting. There are at least two things, though, that make them extremely interesting. One is how the BBO changes over time, say after a major news announcement or after a very large trade when the laws of supply and demand do their thing (more on that in just a bit). The other thing of interest here is trading interest *not* displayed. There may be a prospective buyer, for instance, willing to pay something more than a dollar, or a seller willing to take less than a dollar ten but not wanting to reveal those intentions for some reason or another. The dynamics of the BBO, and the effect of such hidden liquidity, will indeed take up much of the rest of this book. It's what much of the tizzy around high-frequency trading is all about.

There's more to the order book than the BBO or *top of book*. There are also not-quite-best bids and not-quite-best offers maintained on the order book, like this:

... 600 | 0.98 550 | 0.99 500 | 1.00 × 1.10 | 600 1.11 | 800 1.12 | 950 ...

Here we see part of what's known as a *depth of book* view of a sample market. To the left of the BBO are bid prices and corresponding prices successively lower than the best bid of $1.00, and to the right are offer prices and corresponding sizes successively greater than the best offer of $1.10. These off-market quotes sit in the wings, as it were, waiting to go on stage. In the sample market above, for instance, if a seller were to come in and sell 500 securities to the $1.00 bidder, that bid would be removed from the market and the best bid would become 550 bid for 99 cents. (Selling at a bid, by the way, is known as *hitting* the bid. Buying at the offer is known as *lifting* the offer.[15]) Should the seller want to buy more than 500 units, say 600, they would hit the entire $1.00 bid (known colorfully as *whacking* it) and also sell 100 units to the $0.99 bidder.[16,17]

---

[15] Buying at the offer is also known as *taking* the offer.

[16] This is sometimes known as *walking the book*. Some exchanges handle this differently, for example by converting the remaining order quantity to a limit order. But for our purposes, we'll assume this mechanism.

[17] This example assumes, for illustrating this point, that Acme trades only on this exchange. In the United States, were Acme multiply listed, the exchange here would generally be required under Regulation National Market System (NMS) to seek another $1.00 bidder on another exchange before filling the additional 100 shares at $0.99—unless they flashed the order, which is a topic we aren't yet ready dive into, but shall.

NBBO

Most securities trade not at one exchange but at several, so at any given moment, there are several active order books, each at a different exchange, for a given security. Each exchange has its BBO as discussed previously, and sometimes the prices are the same at different exchanges and sometimes not. The *national best bid and offer*, or NBBO, is the highest bid price and lowest offer price from the set of all exchanges.[18] Here's an example of three BBOs and the resulting NBBO:

Exchange A "AEX" BBO 500 | 1.00 × **1.09 | 400**
Exchange B "AEX" BBO **200 | 1.02** × 1.11 | 600
Exchange C "AEX" BBO 700 | 1.01 × **1.09 | 300**
NBBO 200 | 1.02 × 1.09 | 700

NBBO prices became especially relevant in the United States when Regulation NMS took effect in 2005, which mandates (among other things, but chiefly) that any public investor is entitled to trade at the NBBO regardless of the exchange to which their order is sent.

The Market Spread

The difference between a bid price and its corresponding offer price is known as the *spread*.[19] It's also known as the *market width*. The theoretical price in the middle of a spread is known

---

[18] As we use the term *exchange* to include ATSs, it's important to note that dark pools, by definition, do not disseminate quotes and are therefore not generally included in NBBO calculation.

[19] This is not to be confused with the *spread trade*, which we won't get into in this book.

as the midmarket price, or just *midprice*.[20] The spread of a market (along with bid and offer sizes, known as *depth*) is often used as an indicator of its liquidity. There is a nagging lack of consensus on a precise definition of liquidity, but people do tend to recognize it when they see it. In a more liquid market, goods "flow" more easily—there is more trading—than they do in a less liquid market because the prices are better to both buyers and sellers (and there are plenty of goods available to trade at those prices). The key here is that higher bids are good for sellers and lower offers are better for buyers, so tighter spreads indicate a good deal for both sides.

Consider these two hypothetical markets for the same security:

$$5,000 \mid 1.00 \times 1.13 \mid 5,000$$
$$5,000 \mid 1.06 \times 1.07 \mid 5,000$$

The midprice of both of these markets is $1.065 ([1.00 + 1.13]/2). A buyer of 5,000 securities in the first market, however, will pay $5,650, whereas in the second market he or she would pay only $5,350. Likewise, a seller of 5,000 securities receives $5,000 in the first market but $5,300 in the second. The tighter market is clearly better for both buyer and seller. As it turns out, before the advent of decimalization in the U.S. stock market, when the minimum market width was one-eighth of a dollar or 12.5 cents, both buyers and sellers were stuck with markets much like the first one. Now that stocks (and an increasing number of options) are traded in pennies,[21] markets for most popular securities are more like the second case. High-frequency traders take much of the credit for this

---

[20] To calculate the precise midpoint, add the bid and offer and divide the sum by two. You may, of course, get a fractional result.

[21] Some markets allow price increments of well under a penny.

marked improvement in market liquidity, a claim we'll be in a position to evaluate later on.

Price Dynamics

Before long, we'll discuss the market impact of trade orders, or the way in which the mere presence of an order—especially a large one—can itself move market prices "away from the order." A large order (known sometimes as a *block*,[22] or a *size* order) to sell will tend to depress prices; an order to buy will tend to push them up. This phenomenon is central to trading, known intuitively by veteran traders, and one without which one could argue there would be no high-frequency trading in the first place. It all derives from simple rules of supply and demand. The presence of these rules in nonfinancial markets is fairly obvious and intuitive. As demand for something increases, so does its price due to increased competition among its buyers. Demand and price are thus said to be positively correlated. Supply and price, on the other hand, are negatively correlated. As supplies increase, prices decrease due to increased competition among sellers. We see this effect so often one hardly has need to think about it, say with gasoline, when pump prices might rise as summer drivers mass to the highways and fall when oil producers overproduce.

Pressure from the buy-side drives prices up, pressure from the sell-side drives them down. We see the very same thing on the BBO at a securities exchange. An increase in the bid size is going to push up prices—both bids and offers. An

---

[22] There is no fantastic, generally accepted definition of just what constitutes a block trade. Time was, an order for 10,000 shares or more was considered a block, but blockiness really depends on the share price. Ten thousand shares of a stock trading for a few pennies is not a big deal compared to, say, 10,000 shares of Google, which trades as of this writing for more than $500.

TABLE 2.4

Market Dynamics

Time 1	500l1.00 × 1.10l500	Market is balanced with midprice of 1.05.
Time 2	2,500l1.00 × 1.10l500	Bid size increases by 2,000.
Time 3	2,500l1.02 × 1.12l500	Market rebalances at a midprice of 1.07.
Time 4	2,500l1.02 × 1.12l2,500	Offer size increases by 2,000.
Time 5	2,500l1.00 × 1.10l2,500	Market rebalances at a midprice of 1.05.

increase on the offer size does the same thing, only the other direction. Consider the scenario in Table 2.4.

We'll see later on precisely what can happen to move prices in response to increased bid or offer size, but the point here is simply that supply-and-demand dynamics affect the BBO the same way they do the price of gasoline, apples, MP3 players, and so on. Increased demand pushes it up, increased supply pushes it down.[23]

Hidden Liquidity

In the previous example, the increases in size were visible to anyone watching this market, and prices changed as you would expect. Increased demand caused sellers to raise offer prices because they had a clear sign the market would bear it. This, in turn, caused bidders to be willing to pay more. Increased size did the exact opposite.

Imagine now that the party wanting to buy 2,000 for $1.00 had not yet put out the bid but told everyone they intended to, say by tweeting it to everyone at the exact same time. Would you expect market prices to increase? Sure. Sellers had the same exact signal as before, that the market would bear a higher price, just by way of Twitter this time instead of the

---

[23] We'll see how they tend to push too far when we discuss *mean reversion*.

order book. The same would be true if the party wishing to sell 2,000 at the offer similarly communicated their interest by some other means than joining the offer on the book.

The point here that known changes in liquidity, especially substantial ones, as signals of supply relative to demand, will move a market whether visible as in the first case or hidden as in the second.[24]

TRADING

Now that we are acquainted with the securities, the place where they are traded, and the all-important order book, let's consider the act of trading itself. This act begins with the submission of an order. For our purposes, the four essential elements of any order are these:

- Symbol
- Buy or Sell
- Quantity (size)
- Price

Incidentally, there is a well-established convention for expressing a trade order verbally. Were your intention to buy 500 shares at a price of $1.00 each, you would say "one dollar bid for five hundred" (price for size). Were your intention to sell, you would say "five hundred offered at one dollar" (size at price). The relevance of such a thing is obviously diminishing in an age of increasing automation, but it is an interesting exemplification of linguistic efficiency nonetheless, at least for those interested in things such as exemplifications of linguistic efficiency, of which this sentence is certainly not.

---

[24] In the next chapter, we'll discuss *reserve* orders and *iceberg* orders, two other means of hiding liquidity.

While we're on the subject of orders, in addition to specifying the essentials (security, buy versus sell, price, and quantity) you will also specify a qualifier indicating how you wish the order to be handled. Chief among these is whether it is a *market order* (you will pay the best offer or receive the best bid) or *limit order* (you specify the price at which you are willing to trade). A limit order is further qualified by how long the exchange should attempt to fill it. The most common of these qualifications go by names such as *good-till-cancel* (self-explanatory), *good-till-day* (cancel if not filled by close of trading), *immediate-or-cancel* (try to fill at least some now and cancel the rest), and *all-or-none* or *fill-or-kill* (cancel if you can't fill all of it right now). Some exchanges offer subtle variations on these and might use different labels for these qualifiers, but the essence of an order—an expression of an interest to buy or interest to sell—is the same everywhere.

This is also a good point to examine the two fundamental types of sell orders for stock. These are *long sells* (I own the stock and want to sell it) and *short sells* (I borrowed the stock and now want to sell it, and I will buy it back later so I can return it to the lender). It's a distinction that trips people up all the time but is really straightforward once you know their respective justification. The essential reason for selling a security long is to get rid of it, for some purpose or another. The essential reason for selling a security short is to profit from the decline in its price. Example: If I borrow your stock and sell it to the market for ten dollars, and the market price of the stock falls to nine dollars, I can buy it back from the market for nine, return it to you, and keep a one dollar profit; should the market price rise I will, of course, lose money on this trade. Options market-makers, whom we'll discuss soon, are also very active short sellers of stock. They sell short not for speculation but to lock in a profit from the sale or purchase of option contracts, that is, to *hedge* their option positions.

Short selling became more than a bit controversial after the market crash of 2008. Detractors posited that short selling accelerated the slide. They called for the reinstatement of so-called "uptick rules" that allow one to sell short only after a price increase, thus keeping short sellers from piling on when a stock price is in decline. Advocates of short selling position it as an essential tool for investors, ensuring that market prices are accurate indicators of the true value of a stock. When investors believe a stock is underpriced with respect to the fundamental attributes of the company behind it—earning potential, strength of management, market position, and so on—they can buy the stock. As we discussed earlier, increased buying pressure will push the price up until investors believe the price is right—and make those investors a profit as well, motivating them to keep a lookout for such opportunities. Conversely—and crucially if you are a defender of short selling—when investors believe a stock is overpriced, short selling allows them to likewise profit on its correction in the other direction.

Another concept that comes up in any examination of high-frequency trading is the notion of *passive trading* versus *active trading*. To trade passively is to submit an order when you are not certain there is someone ready to take the other side, whereas to trade actively is to submit an order in response to a displayed bid or offer. Consider the 1.00 × 1.10 market. Were you to join this market, by submitting a dollar bid or an order to sell at a dollar ten, you would be passively trading. Submitting even a dollar one bid, or a dollar nine bid, would be passive as there is no displayed interest to sell at any price less than a dollar ten. Same with an order to sell at any price above a dollar. An example of active trading in this market would be to hit the dollar bid or lift the dollar ten offer. In each of those cases, you know there is someone willing to trade at those prices. You are saying, OK, I'll take the other side of that trade. Passive trading is also known as *making liquidity*, and active trading as *taking liquidity*.

When you trade actively (assuming you are filled, because someone may, of course, get their order in before you), you remove liquidity from the market, or take it out, so active trading is also sometimes known as *take-out* trading. HFT firms will employ specialized software programs for just such trading, and these programs are hence known as *take-out engines* or *electronic eyes*. Programs for passive trading are known by names such as *quoting engines, autoquoters,* and *quote streamers*.

TRADERS

While there is only one thing to do at an exchange—trade— there are rather different reasons for doing it. And your reason for trading will greatly influence the manner in which you trade, that is, the precise manner in which you submit bids and offers—your prices and sizes, whether they are passive or active, how you qualify them, when you cancel or modify them, and so on. These trading mannerisms are typically known as *strategies*, and we'll explore those later on. Before we do, and to help us get our arms around this broad topic, we'll identify four types of trader: the *investor*, the *market-maker*, the *arbitrageur*, and the *predictor*. These are archetypes, if you will, sweeping generalizations every one. It is certainly not likely that an actual trader or trading firm will fit into one and only one of these categories. A firm might trade wearing more than one of these hats—subject to rules and regulations that would fill a book of their own. Still, the archetypes will facilitate the making of sense when we get to trading strategies.

The Investor

Investors generally trade because they want to either grow their position in a security or reduce it.[25] The key thing is this: Investors increase or decrease their position in a security for the inherent benefit of doing so. They buy a stock because they think it will appreciate in value, or short it with the opposite view, or sell it out of their portfolio because they no longer expect it to appreciate or appreciate enough for their liking. Whatever. And when our investors do hold a security, they intend to do so for relatively long periods of times—let's say weeks, months, or years. Of course, it's arbitrary to be more exact than that. For people and firms making very short-term "investments" of, say, days or minutes or seconds or milliseconds, we have the predictor category explained later.

Naturally, when investors trade, they want to do so at the best available price—the highest bid if they are selling and the lowest offer if they are buying. Tighter markets are better than wider markets for the investor. And, of course, investors want to keep their transaction costs—exchange and brokerage fees, for example—as low as possible.

Within the investor category, we have both *individual investors* and *institutional investors*. The former is generally an individual person who makes trades directly, say via an online brokerage. The latter makes trades for the benefit of a group of individuals. The group might be the investors in a mutual fund or hedge fund, the future beneficiaries of a pension fund, or some other large group. And the key word is *large*. Institutional orders tend to be far larger than those of individual investors. Another relevant point about institutional investors is their fiduciary duty to their investors,

---

[25] A trade that increases a position is known as an *opening* trade. One that reduces a position is known as a *closing* trade.

that is, their obligation to make the best possible trades for their constituents. This fiduciary duty, and the inherently large sizes of their trades, makes them keenly sensitive to the market impact of their orders and trades as illustrated by our earlier discussion of price dynamics and hidden liquidity. That sensitivity will be apparent when we explore investor trading strategies.

By convention, traders acting as or on behalf of investors tend to be known as *buy-side* traders. The label doesn't work literally, as investors are nearly as likely to sell as they are to buy, but the term persists nonetheless. The term *sell-side* trader usual refers to a trader like our market-maker, whom we'll talk about next, even though they, too, are as likely to buy as to sell.

The Market-Maker

In an ideal market, investors could always trade with other investors. Someone wishing to buy some quantity of stock for their portfolio would always find someone wishing to remove the same quantity from theirs, and vice versa. Indeed, in some markets, for example, those for the most actively traded stocks, this is likely at times to be the case. But for the most part, across the equity supermarket, there is insufficient natural liquidity to always match investors with other investors.[26] This is where the market-maker comes in.

These traders, also sometimes known as *specialists*, stand ready at all times to either buy or sell a security at prespecified—or quoted—bids and offers. Their existence ensures that an investor will always find a counterparty when they wish

---

[26] This is certainly true for options and for less liquid stocks. Futures markets, especially the ones we'll talk about, tend to have abundant natural liquidity such that market-making per se isn't so essential.

to buy or sell. When you look at an order book, then, some of the size may represent the interest of investors and some may represent that of market-makers. In the BBO that follows, for example, 500 of the shares available to buy at $1.10 may be offered by a market-maker with the remaining 100 representing an investor's order to sell. To a prospective buyer, say, it doesn't matter whether the seller is a market-maker or another investor. The only things that matter are price and size. It's also conceivable that at times the entire size behind a bid or offer is presented by a market-maker. Imagine if the 500 one-dollar bids all represented market-maker interest, but only a portion of the 550 bid at 99 cents. In this case, the mere presence of market-makers improves the bid.

... 600 I 0.98 550 I 0.99 500 I 1.00 × 1.10 I 600 1.11 I 800 1.12 I 950 . . .

The pure market-maker has no inherent interest in holding securities. They are said colloquially to be "in the moving business, not storage." The interest of a market-maker is unabashedly simple: they want to buy at one price and sell at some higher price, completing the round-trip, as it were, to earn the difference as a profit. So market-makers work to earn the spread—and the wider the spread the better. This is, of course, the exact opposite of investors, who prefer tighter markets.

If market-makers could always make pairs of offsetting trades, buying low and selling high, there would be no risk. But this is decidedly not the case. Consider the tight (but not at all unrealistic) market that follows:

---

500 I 1.04 × 1.06 I 100

Say market-maker Ken is on both the bid and the offer. Someone lifts his offer with a 100-lot buy order, so he short-sells at the quoted $1.06. Since this represents the entirety of the offer, the BBO changes to, say, this:

500 I 1.04 × 1.07 I 500

He waits for someone to hit his $1.04 bid so he can close out his short position and earn the two-penny spread. While he is waiting, however, the market moves to this:

500 I 1.07 × 1.08 I 500

Dang. Now he finds himself short 100 shares with no easy way to buy them back at a lower price. The best he might do in this market is buy them for $1.07, at a loss of one dollar (100 shares at a $.01 loss per share). Rather than risk going further underwater, he lifts the offer and takes his licks, demonstrating the inherent risk of market-making.

Here's the scenario again, with a happier outcome. Same initial market as before:

500 I 1.04 × 1.06 I 100

Market-maker Ann is on both the bid and the offer. Someone lifts her offer with a 100-lot buy order, so she short-sells at the quoted $1.06. The BBO changes as it did with Ken:

500 I 1.04 × 1.07 I 500

Ann knows she would earn two dollars if and when someone hits her bid. Rather than risk it, however, she improves her quote by a penny. Now the market looks like this:

---

100 | 1.05 × 1.07 | 500

Some seller sees the bargain and snaps it up, hitting her bid and selling her 100 shares for $1.05. She returns those shares to whomever she borrowed them from, closing out her short position. Because she sold at $1.06 and bought at $1.05, she has earned a dollar.

The scenarios so far illustrate the risk market-makers take, risk for which they are compensated when they earn the spread. And if we extend it slightly, it illustrates another dynamic. Say that yet another market-maker, Jason, who is already offering some of the 500 shares at $1.07, sees Ann improve her bid and decides to join her price with a 500-lot bid of his own. The market now looks like this (remember Ann's 100 was taken out):

---

500 | 1.05 × 1.07 | 500

Now an investor order comes in to sell at $1.05, hitting Jason's bid for 100 shares. Like Ann, Jason wants to get out of his position as soon as possible and does so by improving the market to 100 shares at $1.06. He is followed by others for another 400 shares, just as he followed Ann when she improved it to complete her round-trip. Now the market looks like this:

---

400 | 1.05 × 1.06 | 500

That $1.06 offer looks very attractive to a buyer who hits it with a 100-lot buy order. The order is filled by Jason (because he was there first), who earns a dollar profit by selling for $1.06 what he bought for $1.05. Notice the spread? One penny. When we started, the spread was two pennies. Thus, competition among market-makers forced individual market-makers to accept a smaller profit margin, forcing them to improve market prices, with the end result being a better market for investors.

The Arbitrageur

In the physical world, massive objects such as planets draw less massive objects to the center of their mass due to the powerful and persistent force of gravity. Gravity is always there, ready to bring airborne objects back to earth, be they beach balls, baseballs, or buttered toast. In the financial markets, we find a similarly powerful force known as the *law of one price*, the consequence of something known as the *arbitrage pricing theory*, which keeps the prices from straying away for too long from one true price. That true price may, of course, change over time, but at any point in time there is only one.

One of the consequences of this law is that if a given security is traded in multiple markets, and the cost of trading is the same at each market, then at any given time the price must be the same across all markets. If not, a trader known as an arbitrageur can make riskless profits by buying at the lower-priced market and selling at the higher-priced one until the effect of such trading brings prices back together. Imagine the stock PDQ is tradable at two exchanges, and the markets at those exchanges look like this:

Exchange A: PDQ 500 I 1.00 × **1.02** I 500
Exchange B: PDQ 500 I **1.03** × 1.04 I 500

Here we have a so-called *crossed market*, where the bid on one exchange is greater than the offer on another. Ignoring trading costs, an arbitrageur who can simultaneously buy for $1.02 at exchange A and sell at exchange B for $1.03 makes an instant profit of one penny just for spotting the incongruity and trading on it. The actual profit may be less than a penny due to the net cost of making the trades, but it illustrates the point. And the arbitrageur will, of course, trade for as long as he can in this manner, scooping up all those pennies until the markets uncross and look perhaps something like this:

Exchange A: PDQ 500 | 1.00 × 1.03 | 500
Exchange B: PDQ 500 | 1.02 × 1.04 | 500

You can tell already that speed is of the essence when trying to arbitrage like this, because who wouldn't want to make these trades? Speed is important for two reasons. One, there are plenty of arbitrageurs constantly looking for mispricings such as this; the arbitrageur with the fastest order-entry mechanism wins. Two, if the orders are not transmitted and processed at precisely the same time, it's entirely possible that one market or the other will move before both "legs" of the arbitrage are done, erasing the mispricing and leaving the arbitrageur with a position to get out of.

The equity supermarket is chock-full of arbitrageurs looking for mispricings and correcting them—at a profit—just as soon as they possibly can. And they look not just for mispriced individual securities as in the example above, but for mispricings between entirely different securities whose prices should be in alignment. Example: ETFs, or index tracking stocks, must be priced consistently with the indices they track. Take the 500 stocks constituting the S&P 500 index, known as the S&P 500 *basket*. Ignoring transaction costs, the price of a Spider ETF should be always one-tenth that of the S&P 500. If the index, which represents the cost of the basket, is trading at $1,400, then an ETF should cost $140. If it is trading higher than $140, one could in essence short ten shares of the ETF and buy the basket. If it is trading below $140, one could short the basket and buy ten shares of the ETF. In reality, we cannot ignore transaction costs and other practical realities that make arbitraging an EFT against the index basket more difficult than it might seem. But given the profits to be made, there are plenty of arbitrageurs only too happy to figure it out.

An ETF must be priced consistently with its associated basket because both the ETF and the basket will produce identical future cash flows. And this is the real crux of the law of the arbitrage pricing theory. Any two securities or portfolios of securities with identical cash flows must have the same price. This allows arbitrageurs to get very creative in looking for arbitrage opportunities. For example, one can create a very simple portfolio of two option contracts on a stock index whose net payoff is identical to a futures contract on the index.[27] If the synthetic future is priced differently from the real future, arbitrageurs can—and will—erase the difference.

The web of subtle but inviolable pricing relationships among securities in the equity supermarket is vast, complex, and dense. The web moves continuously across time, changing shape and composition but always remaining bound together as one massive market. And just as the border collie keeps a stray animal from getting away from the pack for too long, the arbitrageur aggressively and tirelessly shepherds errant prices back to where they need to be.

---

[27] Say, a so-called "combo" of long SPX call and short SPX put versus a long E-mini S&P futures contract whose delivery price and date match the strike prices and expiration dates, respectively, of the combo.

The Predictor

The arbitrage examples just cited all involve mispricings among two or more securities where the mispricing is apparent when the two securities are evaluated at the same point in time. You can roughly think of another type of trader, which we'll call the *predictor*, as looking for pricing discrepancies across time. As you might expect, these are a bit more challenging to detect. And because nothing is absolutely predictable over time, exploiting these discrepancies is much less of a sure thing when compared to simple arbitrage.

The predictor, known also as a *quantitative trader*, practices not what we might call "static" arbitrage but *statistical arbitrage*. You'll find all manner of definition of statistical arbitrage, but it all comes down to analyzing data over time and using it to make predictions about the future direction of prices, using the mathematics of statistics and probability theory, then making trades based on these predictions. If your predictions come true more often than not—even just slightly more often than not—you make a profit.

Perhaps the most common statistical arbitrage strategy is the so-called *pairs trade*. Here, the predictor identifies two stocks whose prices tend to move together over time. Consider the Coca-Cola Company (KO) and PepsiCo (PEP). You would expect these stocks to move in a similar fashion due to the similarity of their products, and if you examine the price paths of these two stocks together, you will see that is the case.[28] The predictor might analyze these two price paths and quantify—very precisely—the relationship between the KO and PEP moves, perhaps noticing that within some degree of certainty, a change in one is typically followed by

---

[28] Sites like Google Finance make this very easy to do. Just search on KO and then specify PEP in the Compare With field.

a corresponding change in the other within some time frame, with one always tending to lead and the other to lag. Should the predictor see the lead stock jump in price, she might immediately buy the lag stock, expecting it to rise in price. If it does, she can then sell it for a profit. The key word here is *if*, because trends like this are not guaranteed to play out the same way in every case.

The pairs strategy has been exploited for many years now, and some might say that pond is fished out. Whereas correlated stocks might have once taken hours or even days to catch up with each other, the existence of so many pairs traders has shrunk the lag time to almost nothing. But the number of possible mispricings across time, considering the web of relationships among securities in the equity super-market, is vast. In the next chapter, we'll examine a few more and some strategies the predictor might employ to take advantage of them.

The High-Frequency Trader

So where does the much-talked-about high-frequency trader fit into this roughly hewn taxonomy of investor, market-maker, arbitrageur, and predictor? A definitive answer to that reasonable question is elusive—and for no small number of reasons. For starters, there is little rational motivation for the high-frequency trader, whomever he or she is, to talk about it. If the stories of the high-frequency trading bonanza are even somewhat on the mark, you might as well set the wayback machine to 1849 and ask the successful gold miner to show you his stake and let you dig around for awhile. Indeed, the high-frequency trader will be even more pro-tective than the 49er because trading strategies are extraor-dinarily portable. The essential trade secrets in this corner of the financial pantheon are easily contained in the space between the ears of just one knowledgeable employee, with plenty of room to spare.[29]

Aside from this obvious profit protection motive, it's also plausible that some HFT firms may not want anyone to ever know what they did to extract their gold—and to have those actions examined under the klieg lights of ethics and legality, even after their stake is mined out. Lastly, but certainly not leastly, there just may be no good definition to be had. The label *high-frequency trader* itself is an invention of greater interest to those on the outside of the business than on the inside, a manifestation of the natural desire to know in simple terms what's going on inside an inherently complex world, a place where the only act of simplicity on a given day might be the brewing of a pot of coffee.

Despite the definitional difficulty, you won't be too far off the mark to think of the quintessential high-frequency trader as a hybrid market-maker and predictor with awesome technological capabilities. The essential goal of this sell-side trader is the same as market-makers in the days way before the machines took over, that is, to buy on the bid and sell on the offer, buying low and selling high, in order to earn the spread. Due to things like decimalization, advancements in computing technology, and increased competition, however, the high-frequency trader must resort to more innovative, aggressive, and (some would say) predatory strategies than those of traditional market-makers. We'll examine some of those strategies in the next chapter. The high-frequency trader is also more selective than the pure market-maker when it comes to choosing which securities to trade, tending

---

[29] To wit, HFT giant Citadel's 2009 lawsuit against three former employees for allegedly violating noncompetition agreements in their formation of the HFT firm Teza Technologies, this right after Teza hired the former Goldman Sachs employee nabbed for allegedly stealing their HFT secrets, whom they promptly fired. It wasn't a good year for the Teza guys.

to favor those where speed of execution provides an advantage, namely, in the most actively traded stocks.[30]

The high-frequency trader is not the only trader who attempts to leverage technology to his advantage. You'll hear the term *algorithmic trader* (or *black-box trader*) tossed about in the context of high-frequency trading, but, in most cases, this actually refers not to our high-frequency trader but to his buy-side counterpart. The algorithmic trader is more likely than not an institutional investor taking advantage of automation to serve the interests of her constituents. She traditionally leverages computational power not so much for speed of execution (although more and more she certainly is) but to determine things like optimal composition of large portfolios, when to buy and sell stocks, and how to minimize the market impact of her orders.

By now you know, of course, not to take these definitions too strictly. The firm that performs high-frequency trading and/or algorithmic trading as we are now defining it may certainly wear the other trading hats we've talked about. For example, the same firm who does HFT in the most active names may indeed make markets in the less liquid names and is certainly likely to have a system in place to exploit basic arbitrage opportunities. Even the algorithmic trader is likely to consider the statistical arbitrage strategies of the predictor when designing her algorithms.

There is, however, one very imposing limit to how many of these hats a given trading operation can wear at one time. This is the required separation between so-called *customer trading* and *proprietary trading*. The idea here is that a broker-dealer looking to fill a customer's order at the best possible

---

[30] You'll hear that high-frequency traders only trade the top 300 or so names, but nobody can say for certain. And some HFT firms focus on fewer names, others on many more.

price should not at the same time also be placing orders for their own benefit, or "for their own account" as it's known. The temptation to front-run the customer is just too great, or, at a minimum, makes a customer reasonably wonder if she is getting the best possible service from her broker. Firms that do only customer trading, or only proprietary trading, need not worry so much about the separation. But firms that do both—and many Wall Street firms and hedge funds do— must take great care in erecting so-called information barriers between the customer desk and the proprietary desk.

CHAPTER 3

Trading Strategies

Earlier, we organized securities traders into four archetypal categories according to their reason for trading: The investor generally wants to hold securities for comparatively long investment periods. The market-maker wants to earn the bid-ask spread as compensation for the risk of making two-sided markets. The arbitrageur wants to profit by trading mispriced securities, selling the overpriced and buying the underpriced and pocketing the difference. The predictor uses quantitative trading (or statistical arbitrage) techniques to analyze data and use it to make predictions about future price changes, and makes trades to profit from those changes when (and if) those predictions come true. The high-frequency trader, as noted, is essentially a hybrid of the market-maker and short-term predictor.

In this chapter, we'll examine some of the short-term strategies these traders might use to achieve their respective purposes. By *short-term*, we refer specifically to strategies in which time is of the essence. We won't even touch on long-term strategies, such as what type of securities to invest in, how long to hold them, portfolio diversification, and so on. Those can—and do—fill books all on their own.

Do these pages describe all strategies traders use to make all that money we read about? Every one of them? Yes! I mean no. Would that such a book existed. As you would expect, there are plenty more strategies than just these. Trading strategies are the secret sauce of any trading firm. They are the cola recipe, the football playbook—you get the idea. The ones presented here have been around long enough to migrate from one firm to another (traders do change jobs) or to make it into public discourse. And some of them are just plain obvious. You can bet there are strategies designed to outsmart the strategies presented here, and that small armies of well-compensated quantitative types are dreaming up new ones all the time. But we need to start somewhere, right?

For the most part, we'll assume all trading takes place on one stock exchange where there are large numbers of both passive and active traders. We'll also assume the exchange employs *price-time* order priority, in which orders are filled in the order in which they are received by the exchange, with more aggressively priced orders (buy for $1.00) filled before less aggressive ones (buy for $0.90). We'll also assume the exchange follows a *maker-taker* pricing model in which traders who make liquidity (post new bids or offers) are paid a rebate upon passive filling by the exchange as an incentive to trade there, and traders who take liquidity (hit bids or lift offers) pay a fee. Example of making liquidity: The market is 1.00 × 1.10, and Mr. Frick posts a bid improving the market to 1.01 × 1.10. Example of taking liquidity: Ms. Frack hits the $1.01 bid and pays a taker fee of, say, a penny. The exchange pays some of that penny to Mr. Frick.

Both price-time allocation and maker-taker pricing are prevalent on most U.S. stock markets and some U.S. option markets (e.g., NYSE Arca Options and NASDAQ Options Market). Another option pricing model known as customer-priority (e.g., at the CBOE and ISE) charges some transaction fees to professional traders but not to nonprofessionals, or customers. Those same option exchanges also give customers allocation priority over professional traders, hence the name. And just to round out the picture, at the dominant U.S. futures exchange (the CME), both maker and taker each pay a fee regardless of who they are, with member firms generally paying a smaller fee than nonmembers. You might not think the minutiae like fee and rebate policies are even worth bringing up, but they've actually turned into quite a big deal. As we'll see below, for example, when spreads narrow to almost nothing, the rebate can be the only compensation available to a market-maker.

INVESTORS VERSUS MARKET-MAKERS

The first two traders we'll consider are the institutional investor (the so-called buy-side) and pure market-maker (sell-side) and their respective interests and strategies. In practice, our "investor" is likely to be a broker-dealer working on behalf of an actual investor. To keep things simple, we'll not get into the relationship between investors and brokers and abstract the latter out of the picture. No disrespect intended to my friends in the brokerage community, but we simply needn't get into that gray area to understand the essence of high-frequency trading. I think they'll understand.

By "pure" market-maker, we mean one who is working only for the spread and/or rebate and is not also applying arbitrage strategies. In most markets, investors and market-makers are hugely dependent on each other. Investors need market-makers to ensure they will find liquidity (i.e., someone to take the other side of their trades), and market-makers need investors to hit their bids and lift their offers so they can capture spread and/or rebates.[1] But as we saw in the previous chapter, they have diametrically opposite preferences when it comes to the spread: market-makers want it wide and investors want it narrow. As such, investors and market-makers are at natural odds with one another. It's not quite the Hatfields versus the McCoys, but neither is it Fibber McGee and Molly. As in any robust and competitive market, this powerful conflict of interest between investors and market-makers keeps both parties on their respective toes.

We assume our investor is an institutional investor "trading size" for the benefit of her constituents. Much of our discussion pertains in theory to individual investors with small orders, but, for all practical purposes, the large orders (block trades) are getting our attention due to their potential to move a market against the investor. This leads us to the topmost concern of our investor: to make a trade (i.e., find liquidity, find counterparties) while minimizing the market impact of her order. She does not want her order to itself move the market against her—or, more precisely, against the beneficiaries of her work, to whom she has a fiduciary duty to trade at the best possible price. This obligation also means our investor would prefer not to pay the spread. We will assume she is content to pay the market midprice; she would be happier, of course, to trade on her side of the BBO[2] (buy on the bid, sell at the offer) and would definitely prefer not to pay the market spread (buy at the offer, sell on the bid). But the midprice, for our general purposes, would be fine. And naturally, the investor wishes to minimize her transaction costs, such as exchange and brokerage fees.

---

[1] In markets where there is sufficient natural liquidity among investors, that is, pairs of investors whose orders are exactly opposite each other, investors are less reliant on market-makers.

[2] BBO = best bid and offer, as explained previously.

As with the investor, the market-maker has a relatively small number of primary motivators driving his strategies. Paramount among these is risk management. Recall that our market-maker has no inherent interest in holding securities for any longer than he has to. In his perfect world, he would buy at the bid from one party (such as an investor, but, of course, he doesn't care who it is), then immediately sell to another at the offer to get out of his position. Conversely, he would sell at the offer to one investor then complete his round-trip by immediately buying from another at the bid, again with no residual position. He's in the moving business, remember, not storage. But his world is not perfect. As we saw in the previous chapter, the worst thing that can happen for a market-maker is to trade at one price and be forced to pair it off with an inferior trade, i.e., to get "run over" when a market moves against him, before the round-trip is completed, forcing him to sell for less than he paid.

The market-maker is inherently at risk because there is always some lag time before he can get the round-trip done, and prices move unpredictably during the course of that lag. As you might expect, the market-maker wants to maximize his compensation for this inherent and substantial risk of making two-sided markets. If he sells a security, he wants to buy it back at not just a low price but the lowest possible price he can get. If he buys, he wants to sell it at the highest possible price. This is motivated not simply by profit maximization (although there is that) but also by compensating for the inevitable bad trades, which even the best market-maker will experience from time to time and which take money directly out of his pocket. He'd like to earn it back on other trades.

Both of these motivations—avoiding the run-over and maximizing compensation—force a market-maker to be insanely sensitive to something we've already talked about: large orders not yet visible to the market. Size orders move the market. And just as the investor wants to keep her size orders close to the vest for as long as possible, the market-maker would like very much to know about those orders so he can get out of their way, or—when permissible—get in front of them (more on this when we get to strategies).

We'll talk more about speed later on, but it's worth noting already the respective importance of transaction time to the investor and market-maker. Simplifying just a bit, by transaction time we mean the length of time it takes to get the orders (in the case of an investor) or the quotes (in the case of a market-maker) into or out of the market. Both investor and market-maker want their orders and quotes into and out of the market as quickly as possible for roughly the same reasons: to take advantage of desirable prices before they are gone and to get out of the way when the market moves against them. The difference is in the sheer number of transactions involved. An institutional investor may be working one order at a time—or maybe a handful, or even a hundred. But a typical market-maker will have several hundred or even thousands of quotes in the market simultaneously. An options market-maker may have *hundreds* of thousands of quotes out there, each one of them a binding commitment to trade. One swift and unexpected market move can be painful for the investor but catastrophic to the market-maker. The investor and market-maker both care about speed, but the market-maker cares quite a lot more.

INVESTOR STRATEGIES

Working an order is the term of art for an investor who employs one strategy or another, or some combination of strategies, to execute a desired trade on the most favorable terms. An investor who uses software to automatically work orders is sometimes known as an *algorithmic trader*. It's an imperfect term, not to be taken literally, because *algorithm* is just a jazzy term for a well-defined set of instructions for completing some task. The routine for starting your car is an algorithm. So is my special recipe for margaritas. And so are the things market-makers do—but they aren't considered algorithmic traders. Go figure. So because investors using automated trading techniques are known as algorithmic traders, the strategies here are also known as *algorithmic strategies*. They are also sometimes known as *automated trading, black-box trading,* or *robo trading* strategies (despite, again, those terms doing quite a good job of describing what a market-maker does as well).

Market Order

The easiest strategy for our investor when she wants to trade is to simply place a market order, an order to trade at the posted bid (for a sale) or offer (for a buy) (see Figure 3.1, where the circles, squares, triangles, and associated quantities represent different traders and their order sizes). The downside here is a virtual guarantee of paying the market spread, which we've already noted is something our investor would prefer not to do. Some investors may be perfectly willing to pay the spread, for example, if they are more interested in getting a stock out of their portfolio than the price they receive for it.

If it's a market order to buy, the investor expresses a willingness to pay the current best offer and hopefully does so. If it's a market order to sell, she is willing to do so at the current best bid and hopefully does so. I say "hopefully" because there is no guarantee her order will arrive in time to actually trade at the market price. Another order may get in ahead of hers, taking out the bid or offer, or the bids and offers she sees at the time she places her order may be modified by the time her market order arrives. So even for this most trivial case, speed of execution can make a difference, especially when the inves-

FIGURE 3.1

Investor Strategy: Market Order

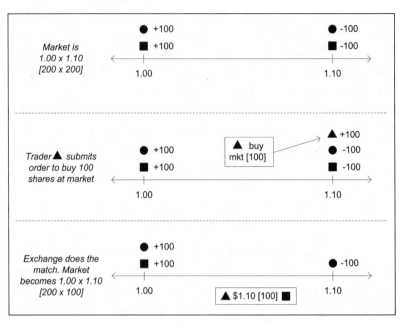

tor believes the market is trending away from her and will continue to do so. It's possible, of course, that market prices could move in her favor before the market order is filled.

Before we leave market orders, what do you suppose would happen were an investor to place a massive market order, say to buy 100,000 shares, in an NBBO market with only 1,000 offered? It's likely the exchanges will let the order "walk the book," filling increasingly high offer prices until the buy order is filled. Such an order would whack several layers of offers, buying from passive liquidity providers at very attractive prices to them (but not so attractive to the buyer). Those providers would then be only too happy to improve the bid in an effort to complete their round-trips. Bottom line, the massive order to buy would raise the market midprice just as the laws of supply and demand suggest it should.

The remaining investor strategies have the investor posting limit orders, or orders with a specified trade price, as discussed in the last chapter.

Poke for Bargains

As we'll see when we get to market-maker strategies, it's not uncommon for liquidity providers to post not their actual best bids and offers but their next best or even next next best. A market-maker may be on both sides of, say, a 1.00 × 1.10 market but actually be willing to buy for $1.01 and sell for $1.09.

An investor can take advantage of this common situation to try to do at least slightly better than paying the market spread. To buy in a 1.00 × 1.10, she can submit an order[3] to buy for, say, $1.09 (see Figure 3.2). If there's someone out there actually willing to trade at that price with sufficient size but just not showing it, she automatically does one penny better than a market order. Even better, she can price the order at, say, $1.05 and see what happens. (This isn't so unrealistic, as there are plenty of times a market-maker will "trade at value" or roughly the midprice to complete a round-trip.) If that order comes back empty, she can work her way out one penny at a time, shooting orders for $1.06, $1.07, and so on until she gets a fill. In the worst case, she may end up paying the market offer, which is no worse than a market order, assuming it hasn't moved away from her while she was shopping for improvement.

Join the Makers

Ideally, of course, the investor will buy at the market bid or sell at the offer. And there's no fundamental reason she can't try, by

---

[3] To detect reserve orders (explained more fully later), this could be an IOC, or immediate-or-cancel, order.

FIGURE 3.2

Investor Strategy: Poke for Bargains

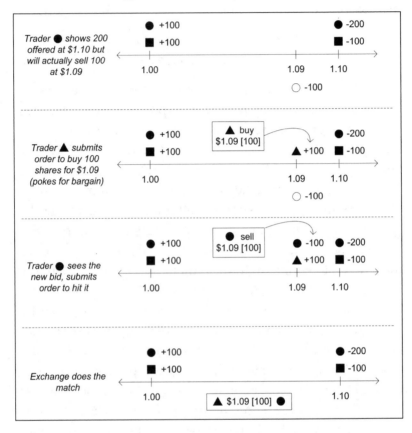

sending a limit order to buy at the current best bid price or sell at the current best offer (see Figure 3.3). Now she's joined the market-makers, attempting to trade passively. When and if a matchable order arrives, she may get a fill. In an exchange with price-time allocation, she will, of course, have to wait her turn and factor that into the decision whether to use this strategy.

A crucial consideration when contemplating joining the market is the current balance of the market with respect to size. If a market is 250 I 1.00 × 1.10 I 5,000 (an extremely asymmetric market just to make this point) and you wish to sell,

FIGURE 3.3

Investor Strategy: Join the Makers

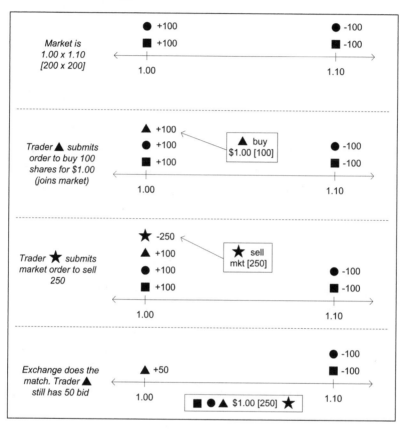

you may not want to bother joining the offer given the number of liquidity providers you'll be competing with for buy orders. But if you wish to buy in this market, you may very well want to join the bidders using the same rationale, this time potentially in your favor. A related consideration is the market impact of your order (i.e., the possibility of moving the market away from you merely by joining it). More on this phenomenon when we get to market-maker strategies.

Incidentally, broker-dealers who offer VWAP pricing guarantees are likely to consider join-the-makers strategies all the time. VWAP (pronounced "vee-wop") stands for *volume weighted average price*, which you can think of very roughly as an average midprice over some time period (a related concept is TWAP, or *time weighted average price*). For example, in our 1.00 × 1.10 market, a broker may guarantee an execution at $1.05 or $1.06 or some other midmarket price to their customer, confident he can use strategies like our investor strategies to trade at that price.

The next strategies deal with what is clearly the most daunting challenge for the institutional investor: how to minimize the market impact of her orders. In each case, the order sits on the book for matching purposes but is invisible, in whole or part, to observers of the market.

Reserve Orders

Some markets allow an order to be placed in the book but not displayed. For example, a market displayed as 700 l 0.99 500 l 1.00 × 1.10 l 500 1.11 l 900 may in reality not be a dollar bid for 500 shares, but for 900 shares. That is, there is a dollar bid—in reserve—for 400 shares (see Figure 3.4). A market order to sell, say, 700 shares will fill entirely with the $1.00 price. Were there no bids in reserve, the market order would fill 500 with a price of $1.00 and 200 with a price of $0.99.

Iceberg Orders

A variation on the reserve order is the *iceberg order*, also known as *hidden-size orders*. Here, the exchange displays only some of an order size and holds the remainder in reserve. For example, a market displayed as 1,200 l 0.99 600 l 1.00 × 1.10 l 500 1.11 l 900 may in reality not be a dollar bid for 600, but, say, for 3,500, with 2,900 of those shares hidden (see Figure 3.5). In other words, there is an order to buy 3,000

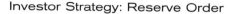

FIGURE 3.4

Investor Strategy: Reserve Order

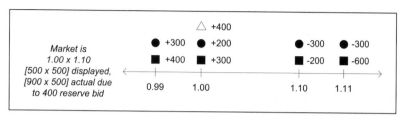

for one dollar but the investor has instructed the exchange to only display 100 at a time. When the 100 bid is hit, the exchange replenishes the bid with another 100 until the entire 3,000 lot order is filled. Note also that if someone hits the bid with more than 600 shares, the exchange will usually fill from the reserve size (the 2,900 hidden in this case) until those shares are gone, as opposed to filling at the inferior displayed price, in this case, $0.99.

Time Slicing

As with the iceberg order, the idea here is to display only a portion of an order size so that a single large order appears to the market in "chunks" of seemingly unrelated orders. With a typical iceberg order, a new chunk is displayed as soon as the displayed one trades. With time slicing, a new chunk is dis-

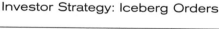

FIGURE 3.5

Investor Strategy: Iceberg Orders

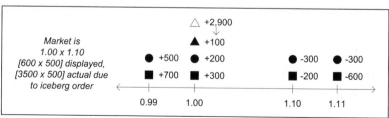

played after the displayed one trades and after some interval of time, say, two seconds, has passed. (To help avoid detection, smart time slicers make this a random interval.) Again, this is repeated until the entire order is filled or the remaining order is cancelled.

MARKET-MAKER STRATEGIES

Recall the pure market-maker has no fundamental interest in holding a security and trades only to earn the bid-ask spread (or, at a minimum, as we'll see, a rebate). In a perfect world, he would simultaneously sell at his offer and buy at his bid all day and go home each night a very happy fella. In reality, he has to work quite a bit harder than that.

Wait for the Other Side

Just as the market order was the base-case strategy for our investor, the simplest strategy for the market-maker once someone has traded with him is to simply wait passively for someone to trade on the other side of his market. If someone hits his bid, obligating him to buy, he then waits for someone to lift his offer so he can sell. Or, if someone lifts his offer, obligating him to sell, he then waits for someone to hit his bid so he can buy. Note that he need not own a security to sell it. He can offer it short. In general, he must follow the same rules as everyone else before he can sell short—locate a lender, mark his offer as a short, and so on—but the point is it's no big deal if, say, his very first trade of the day, when he has no position, is the result of someone lifting his offer.

We already know the risk of this strategy, and it's a big one, so few market-makers are likely to just wait like this. If the market moves against him while waiting, then he gets hosed. If he buys before the market tanks, he's likely to sell for less than he paid. If it rallies after he's sold, he's likely to have to buy for more than he received from the sale.

Lean Your Market

The idea here is that after someone trades with you, you then improve the other side of your market to increase the likelihood of a fill there and degrade the side you just traded on to decrease the likelihood of increasing your exposure. If someone hits your bid, you then improve your offer and degrade your bid. If they lift your offer, you improve your bid and degrade your offer. Biasing your market in this manner is known as *leaning* your market in accordance with your current position and what you want to achieve. A market-maker's position is known as his *inventory*, and this sort of leaning is an example of *inventory exposure management*. As mentioned before, market-makers rarely trade in neat pairs of trades with one trade perfectly offsetting the other. The more likely situation is an accumulation of trades on one side or the other of a market. As an inventory grows, the market-maker is likely to increase his lean accordingly to flatten things out.

Scratch for the Rebate

If a market-maker knows he will receive a rebate of, say, one dollar whenever his 1,000-lot quote trades,[4] and the market spread is very narrow, he may be willing to do a so-called *scratch* trade to complete a round-trip. For example, assume his market is 1,000 | 1.00 × 1.01 | 1,000 and he represents the entire offer size, and someone lifts that offer. He can then

---

[4] As of March 2009, the standard NYSE maker rebate was $0.001 per share, or $1 per thousand shares as in our example here. High-volume market-makers can earn a substantially larger rebate.

improve his bid to \$1.01, shifting the market to, say, 1,000 | 1.01 × 1.02 | 1,000 and wait for his bid (where he just sold) to get hit, thus collecting rebates on both the sale and subsequent purchase. Assuming he traded his full thousand lots each time, he's made two dollars despite having bought and sold for the same price.

Hide Your Best Prices

A market-maker does not have to indicate the very best prices at which he is willing to trade. You can instead post bids and offers slightly worse than your best bids and best offers, then watch the market for incoming orders at better prices and actively take them out. When you see such an order at a price you are willing to trade, then—and only then—do you submit an order to take out the order. Say you are participating on both sides of a 500 | 1.00 × 1.10 | 500 market but are actually willing to buy for \$1.01 or sell for \$1.09. Should a limit order to sell for \$1.01 appear on the book (say, from an investor poking for bargains), you will immediately submit an order to buy at \$1.01 to take it out. The idea here is to trade passively with one market while simultaneously to trade actively at an improved market.

Why not simply post your 1.01 × 1.09 market? By leaving your quoted markets wide, should a market order to sell arrive and you are on the BBO, you are clearly better off having bid \$1.00 than \$1.01. In other words, you can keep your visible market wider for market order fills and take advantage of your hidden, tighter market to take advantage of limit orders at better-than-market prices.

Take Out Slow Movers

This strategy illustrates why passive trading is, all else being equal, riskier than active trading. The setup here is identical to the previous strategy but comes into play when prices move quickly and when some market-makers are faster than others—which is pretty much always. As before, your passive market is slightly wider than your active market at all times. If your active market is one penny inside your passive market and your quotes change, your active market prices change as well. You're basically done. Now, when the market moves quickly and you are moving your quotes to get out of the way, you just might find someone's passive orders on your way out that will kick off your active trading prices.

Say you are participating passively on both sides of a 1.00 × 1.03 market, alongside a bunch of other passive traders, and your active market is 1.01 × 1.02 (see Figure 3.6). Say the market spikes and you change your passive market to 1.02 × 1.05 (as do most but not all of the other passive traders) and your active market to 1.03 × 1.04—but there is still one passive trader, slower than the rest of you, offering $1.03. Your active market will interact with that offer.

Note the tighter active market is not a strict requirement here. One can interact with a slow passive trader with your own, new, passive market. The tighter active market simply allows you to do all this with smaller market shifts.

Penny Jump

When the market-maker accumulates a position, he is at a constant risk of being unable to complete the round-trip at a profit. Worse, should the market move fast enough against him before he can close his position, his losses are essentially unbounded. This risk may keep him from quoting as aggressively as he otherwise would. To mitigate this risk and thereby make himself more aggressive, the market-maker can watch for relatively large increases on either side of the BBO and use those quotes to put a floor on potential losses, or a safety net if you will—if he can move very quickly.

FIGURE 3.6

Market-Maker Strategy: Take Out Slow Movers

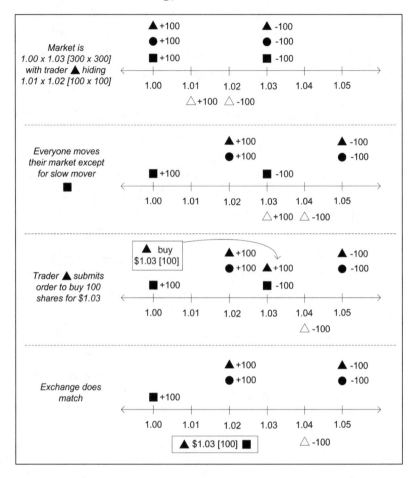

Say the market is 200 | 1.01 × 1.03 | 200, then changes to 3,200 | 1.01 × 1.03 | 200 (see Figure 3.7). You know there is someone willing to buy 3,000 for $1.01. (Ignore for now that you might also treat this like an elephant, explained next.) With this contingency in mind, you improve your bid by one penny to $1.02 (hence the term *penny jumping*), and others hit your bid. You are careful not to buy more than 3,000. Should the market rally to 1.03 × 1.05, you can complete your round-

FIGURE 3.7

Market-Maker Strategy: Penny Jump, Rally

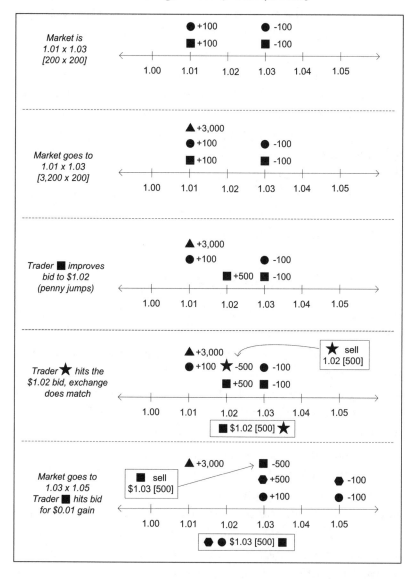

trip (assuming there is sufficient size) at a $0.01 profit by hitting the $1.03 bid. You might wait to see if the market goes higher before closing your position, increasing your profit.

On the other hand, should markets not rally and enough time elapses that you would rather cut your losses than wait, you can sell to the $1.01 bidder, who has backstopped your losses to one penny (see Figure 3.8).[5] This assumes, of course, that the 3,000 are still bid by the time you need to close. As such, superior execution time is crucial here because you want to do all of this before your backstop bidder has an opportunity to modify or cancel his order. While this strategy is known as penny jumping, in markets with subpenny price increments, one obviously need not jump an entire penny for this strategy to work. In fact, you need only improve by the minimum price change. If the minimum price change is, say, $0.001, then the "penny" jumper in our example need only improve the market bid to $1.001.

Push the Elephant

In the previous chapter, we noted the natural tendency of increases in demand to push prices up and of increases in supply to likewise depress prices. This strategy illustrates that concept. Say a market is 500 I 1.00 × 1.01 I 500, then it goes suddenly to 5,500 I 1.00 × 1.01 I 500. The massive joiner here (the elephant) clearly has a huge appetite. He wants to buy 5,000 securities and is joining the bid rather than paying the spread with a market order. If you as a market-maker assume the elephant is willing to pay more than $1.00 (not an unreasonable assumption), you can lift the entire $1.01 offer and improve the bid to $1.01 (see Figure 3.9). Now the market is 1.01 × 1.02. If the elephant still wants to buy, he must improve his bid. If he does, you do the same as before: lift the $1.02 offer and improve the market bid to $1.02, again pushing the elephant to improve his bid.

---

[5] Because this strategy has unlimited upside and limited downside, its payoff is not unlike that of a call option.

FIGURE 3.8

Market-Maker Strategy: Penny Jump, No Rally

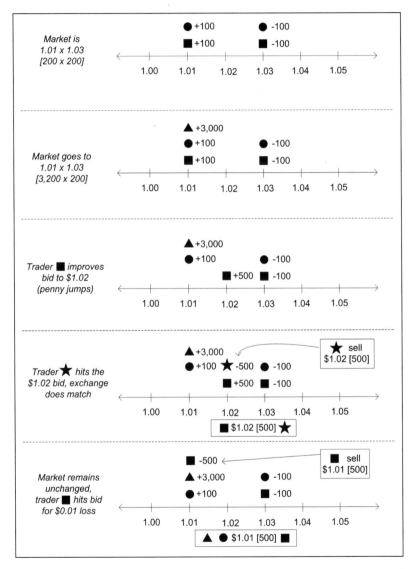

This can go on for some time. Your hope here is that at some point the elephant will be bidding more than you have paid for your shares, say $1.05, and you can hit those bids,

FIGURE 3.9

Market-Maker Strategy: Push the Elephant

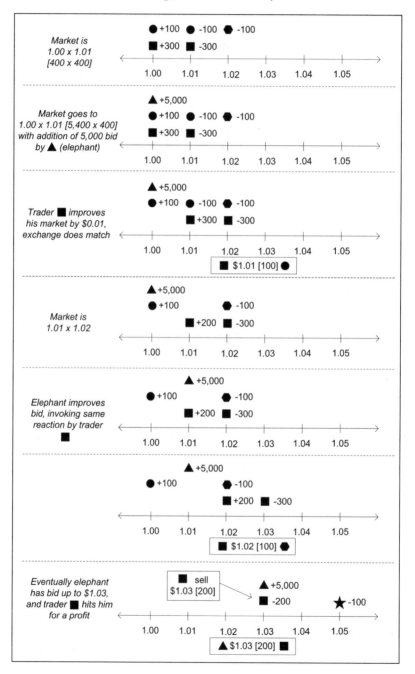

selling him back at a profit the shares you accumulated while trading on the way up. It's not a foolproof strategy, of course, because the elephant can cancel his order at any time and you may have to sell some or all of your shares at a loss. But if the elephant truly wants to buy and is willing to bid up, you can do just fine.

We used a large, elephant-size order to illustrate this strategy, but there is, of course, no clear definition of what is elephantine and what is not. In theory, even a one-lot[6] applies pressure to a market, although in practice that's not likely to be the case. How big an order can be used to trigger a strategy like this one? It's relative to the displayed size, of course. Joining a market with a thousand shares when there are already ten thousand shares displayed will clearly not have the effect of adding a thousand shares to a displayed size of one hundred.

How likely is the elephant to move its prices, and by how much? Deciding how large an order can move a market and by how much, and statistical probabilities for expected moves by the elephant, are good examples of the very hard data analytics work required to make a go of strategies like this and might require the analysis of mountains of historical data, testing, and trial and error. Over time, however, the sophisticated market-maker might find himself with a quite usable model for answering these questions on the fly.

Isn't This Front-Running?

Pushing the elephant might seem like the illegal practice known as front-running, in which someone modifies their trading behavior—based on knowledge of a new and unfilled order—to gain in some way at the expense of the party behind the order. At first blush, that is precisely what seems to be

---

[6] An order for one share of stock, or one option or futures contract.

going on here. But defenders of practices like this would no doubt zero in on the word *knowledge* and change it to *nonpublic knowledge*. They would assert (or have their lawyers assert, in language much more legally impressive than this) that modifying trading behavior in response to public knowledge of a new order is fair game. In this case, the elephant made his presence known to everyone. Anyone participating in this market had an opportunity to react—to "get in front of the order," as it were—in ways that served their own interests and in keeping with the natural rules of supply and demand. Illegal front-running, the defenders would likely continue, entails the modification of one's trading behavior in response to nonpublic information about new orders.

As an example of a blatantly illegal front-run, say a market is 500 | 1.00 × 1.03 | 500. (For illustration purposes, we assume there is only one exchange.) A broker gets a call from a customer asking him to place a market order to buy 500 shares. Before submitting the order, the broker calls a buddy and tells him a market order for 500 shares is on the way. The buddy buys up all the shares offered at $1.03 and joins the new market offer at $1.04. The market order to buy arrives. The buddy sells his 500 shares, the ones he just bought for $1.03, to the unwitting customer for $1.04. As the customer order was known only to the broker and nobody else, this kind of front-running is clearly not kosher.

The next strategy may also smell like front-running at first whiff, but even in this case, the market-maker is using publicly available information to deduce the presence of the hidden order. Check it out and see if you agree.

Tow the Iceberg

As we know, an investor can try to avoid the fate of the elephant by using the iceberg strategy, presenting her order in small pieces so as not to reveal the full extent of her interest. The savvy market-maker, however, can look for signs of an iceberg and treat it as he would an elephant.

Say a market is 500 | 1.02 × 1.07 | 300. A buyer comes along and lifts the $1.07 offer for 300 shares. The offer immediately refreshes, keeping the market unchanged. A moment or so later, it happens again: some buyer whacks the offer, which immediately refreshes. The market-maker sees this (by watching the data feed) and assumes the $1.07 offer is the tip of an iceberg with some remaining quantity still in reserve. He makes an educated guess based on past observations that there are at least 2,000 shares still below the waterline. Now he does pretty much what he does to elephants (this time on the other side of the market since the iceberg is an order to sell). He attempts to sell (short) as market prices decline— indeed to *cause* market prices to decline—then buy them back (close the short position) when prices are lower.

He starts by whacking the $1.02 bid (removing it from the market) and improving the offer to $1.06, a penny better than the iceberg limit price. The market is now 1.01 × 1.06. If the iceberg offer improves to, say, $1.05, he does it all again: whack the $1.01 bid and improve the offer to $1.04. And so on. At some point, the iceberg order is presumably filled and the market bottoms out, say, at 0.96 × 1.00. He lifts the $1.00 offer to close out his accumulated short position, buying for one dollar what he just sold for $1.01 and $1.02.

Unfair? Nefarious? Attempting to move prices after you know there is an order? It might seem that way, but unlike the elephant scenario, in this case, the market-maker doesn't really know there is an iceberg order out there. He suspects it—perhaps with a high degree of statistical probability based on previous experience—but might still be wrong. And if he is, he can find himself in a losing position (e.g., be unable to close out the short at a profit).

Predatory Detection?

In the preceding scenario, the market-maker used public information—the repeated refreshing of the lifted offer—to infer the presence of the iceberg. Let's assume for now we all agree that much is fair. When he improves the offer to $1.06, however, getting in front of the $1.07 seller to deny the seller the opportunity to trade at that price, is that fair? Hard to say.

What if he took things a step further and tried to figure out how low the seller was willing to go by spraying the market with IOC orders to buy at different price levels—one at $1.06, another at $1.05, another at $1.04, and so on, to see what happened? If the $1.06 and $1.05 orders filled and the $1.04 cancelled, he might safely infer that the seller would go no lower than $1.05 and use that knowledge to his advantage as he took his next steps. Some would argue, convincingly, that to submit such an exploratory trade order—with no other purpose than to detect someone's hidden price limit—crosses the boundary between innovation and predation. It reeks especially badly if the predator can act more swiftly than the prey, for example, if the $1.05 bulk seller were technologically incapable of modifying or canceling the order before the order was filled by the better equipped party.

At the moment (early 2010), it appears that practices like elephant pushing, iceberg towing, and even IOC liquidity detection are compliant with existing regulations—or at least in a gray area in which high-frequency traders are willing to take the benefit of the doubt. Whether things stay this way remains to be seen.

Jump the Delta

Market-makers in options have the same fundamental goal as market-makers in stocks: buy a security at one price and sell it at a higher price, earning the spread as a profit.[7] For a number of reasons, including the sheer number of option contracts available for trading, options market-makers, once they make a trade, only rarely have an opportunity to lay off the risk (complete the round-trip) with another option trade. Instead, they attempt to lock in a profit or *hedge* their option trades by trading other carefully selected products, starting with trading a certain number of shares of the underlying stock (e.g., after trading an option on Microsoft, they immediately trade Microsoft stock). The stock portfolio, if maintained properly over time, can act as one component of a *synthetic option* whose value moves to some degree in an equal and opposite manner of the option trade it is hedging. This is known as *delta hedging*, as the number of shares the options market-maker must trade is given by a sensitivity measure known as *delta*.[8]

The market-maker in the underlying stock can use his knowledge of this procedure to his advantage by getting in front of these delta hedges. The basic idea is to watch for large

---

[7] Options are priced in dollars and cents just as stocks are, but options traders often use a measure known as *implied volatility* as a proxy for price. Hence, making markets in options is sometimes known as *volatility arbitrage* or *scalping vol*.

[8] *Delta* indicates how the price of an option changes as the price of the underlying security changes and can thus be used to tell the options market-maker how many shares of stock to maintain to offset changes in the option price. Delta hedging is not the only hedging requirement of an options market-maker, but it's a crucial one. Another of the sensitivities known as *the Greeks* is *vega*, which proscribes how an option price changes as does the volatility of the underlying security. *Rho* measures sensitivity to changes in interest rates, *theta* to changes in time. And rounding out the bunch is *gamma*, which indicates how delta changes with respect to changes in the underlier. Vega and gamma can only be hedged with other options. Rho can be hedged with an interest rate futures contract such as the Eurodollar. For the mathematically curious, each of the Greeks is a partial derivative associated with the celebrated Black-Scholes partial differential equation, from which the Black-Scholes option-pricing formulas are derived.

option trades, figure out which side the market-maker is on, calculate the delta of the option trade about to hit the market, and then get in front of it. For example, the stock market-maker sees in the options market data feed a trade "print" for 5,000 put options[9] on stock XYZ. The strike price on those options is roughly the same as the current market price for XYZ stock, so he knows this is an *at-the-money* option, which, by definition, has a delta of around 50. The option trade price was executed near the current offer price for that option, so the stock market-maker can deduce that the options market-maker sold (or wrote) the option.

To hedge a written put option, one must short-sell the stock. The delta here is 50, the option trade was for 5,000 contracts, each of which has 100 shares of stock as its underlier, so the options market-maker must sell 250,000 shares of XYZ stock (0.50 × 100 × 1,000). Because options market-makers are often willing to pay the market spread, the most common delta hedge order is a market order. Say the market for XYZ stock is 25.50 × 25.60. The stock market-maker—if he acts very quickly, more quickly than the options market-maker—can whack the $25.50 bid and bid $25.49. When the option hedge order to sell at market arrives, it fills at $25.49 and our lightning-fast stock market-maker gets to buy for $25.49 what he just sold for $25.50.

INVESTOR STRATEGIES REDUX

With market-makers applying strategies like penny jumping and iceberg towing and who knows what else, is there any hope for the investor? Sure there is. Just because market-

---

[9] A *put* option gives its buyer the right, but not the obligation, to sell the underlying security in the future at a specified strike price. A *call* option gives its buyer the right to buy the underlier.

makers like to game investors, there's no reason investors can't game them right back or at least foil their attempts—within the confines of the law, of course. For example, one can avoid having one's iceberg towed by not looking so much like an iceberg in the first place—by randomizing the size of the exposed portion of the order and the frequency with which orders are refreshed. And if you are fast, it's not difficult at all to bluff the penny jumper. If you really want to buy, for instance, you may be able to get the penny jumpers out of your way by joining not the bid but the offer, letting the penny jumper get in front of you, then canceling the offer and removing his safety net. While he is scrambling to manage his new risk, you can be on the other side of the market doing your buying.

There's no reason, of course, that the smarts and technologies used by the sell-side high-frequency traders can't be used for the benefit of buy-side mutual funds, insurance companies, and other institutional investors. Firms such as Pipeline Trading Systems, for example, are attempting to do just that. They know the HFT strategies extremely well and develop counterstrategies designed to foil them. For example, they do something like the iceberg strategy, but only stay at one exchange until the first few orders are filled. Then they move the remainder of the iceberg to another market and do the same thing again, all before the high-frequency traders know what's going on and move prices away from them, all at the same cutthroat speeds.

ARBITRAGE STRATEGIES

We've already seen an example of perhaps the easiest arbitrage strategy, deployable when the same stock is available on two different exchanges in a crossed market. Stock PDQ was offered at $1.02 on one exchange and bid for $1.03 on another. The arbitrageur simply lifted the $1.02 offer and hit the $1.03 bid and pocketed the penny difference. It really is that simple, and the money here is virtually free, which explains why opportunities like this typically disappear in less time than it takes a bolt of lightning to hit the ground.

The total profit here is limited, of course, by the number of shares available at the crossed price as well as the cost of making the trade. If, in our example, there are 10,000 shares offered at $1.02 and 2,000 bid for $1.03, then the most you will earn is $20.[10] This profit margin, as all of our arbitrage examples do, assumes that the cost of making this pair of trades does not exceed the arbitrage profit. Should the total cost (exchange fees, etc.) to the arbitrageur exceed a penny, in this case, there is no point making the trade.

This, in fact, is a huge impediment to arbitrage in practice—especially to retail traders who pay relatively large brokerage fees to get their trades done. High-volume arbitrageurs make substantial investments to keep their marginal transaction costs extremely low, say, by purchasing trading rights on multiple exchanges, which allows them to forego brokers. And you can bet your last simoleon that plenty of HFT firms have invested millions of theirs in setting things up to do just that. As a result, stocks and ETFs (which can be arbitraged in virtually the exact same way as stocks) are likely to be priced consistently across all markets where they trade.

The arbitrage opportunities in the equity security supermarket are not limited to individual stocks in crossed markets. Arbitrage is not only possible when the same security is available at different prices on different markets at the same time. Arbitrage is possible between any two securities and/ or portfolios of securities whose prices are related in such a

---

[10] $2,000 \times \$0.01$.

way that they must move together. And there are just gobs of such securities in our supermarket.

ETF Versus Basket

Consider the Spider ETF (symbol SPDR), whose value at any time, as we know, is derived from the total current value of the basket of stocks comprising the S&P 500 index. Imagine owning a portfolio of long positions in each of those 500 stocks. Naturally, whenever the value of any one of those stocks changes, so does the value of the portfolio. It similarly changes when the stocks pay dividends. Now imagine holding a long position in a Spider ETF. Its value will also change as the S&P 500 stocks change value or pay dividends.

As such, the arbitrageur here will carefully track the moment-by-moment values and dividend payments of the 500 stocks in the basket, calculate from those observations what the Spider value should be, and compare it to actual market prices of the Spider. Then he looks for a crossed market. If he sees the net market bid of the Spider (i.e., the price he can sell it for) exceed the net market offer of the basket (the price he can buy it for), he sells the Spider and buys the basket. If the net bid of the basket exceeds that of the Spider, he buys the Spider and sells the basket.

There are all sorts of ETFs available with new ones issued all the time, each one of them a new arbitrage opportunity. The more popular, broad-based index ETFs include not only the Spider for the S&P 500 index, but also the QQQQ for the NASDAQ-100 index and the IWM for the Russell 2000 index. Popular ETFs for smaller indices include the EEM Emerging Market Index and XLF, which tracks a number of stocks from the financial sector.

The effect of transaction speed on the success or failure of this strategy is obvious. This arbitrage works only if the arbitrageur can get filled on the two orders—and one of them may be an order to trade 500 different stocks—before prices move away from him (i.e., before the relative prices of the ETF and basket converge). And with more than one firm looking feverishly for this arbitrage, being a relatively obvious one, he'll have to move faster than anyone else does.

In reality, many brokerages will allow you to trade baskets with a single order or to easily convert an ETF to a basket or vice versa. They charge for such services, of course, so those costs need to be factored in when deciding whether the arbitrage will actually be profitable. ETF arbitrage is trickier than single-stock arbitrage, no doubt about it. But it can be done, and like any arbitrage that can be done, it is done—ferociously.

Futures Versus Basket; Futures Versus ETF

Because the value of an index futures contract is ultimately derived from the values of the stocks in the underlying index, this contract can be arbitraged in much the same way as the ETF. And in fact, the futures contract can be arbitraged against the ETF. Table 3.1 shows some of the more common index futures, the exchange where they trade, and associated ETFs (which trade in multiple stock markets).

Futures Versus Futures

Some futures contracts are easily arbitraged against each other. For example, the CME lists not only the ES (*the mini*) but also the SP (*the big*), which is different from the ES primarily in its contract multiplier of $250 versus $50 for the ES. Another difference is that during trading hours, the SP is only traded in open outcry. After hours, however, the SP can be traded on the CME's electronic platform known as

TABLE 3.1

Futures Contracts and Corresponding ETFs

Exchange	Futures	ETF
Chicago Mercantile Exchange (CME)	S&P 500 Futures (SP) E-mini S&P 500 Futures (ES)	SPDR
Chicago Mercantile Exchange (CME)	NASDAQ-100 Futures (ND) E-mini NASDAQ Futures (NQ)	QQQQ
Chicago Mercantile Exchange (CME)	Dow Futures (DJ) E-mini Dow Futures (YM)	DIA
Intercontinental Exchange (ICE)	Russell 2000 Index Mini Mini Futures (TF)	IWM

Globex. As such, it is relatively easy to automatically monitor the prices of the ES and SP and look for times when they diverge. The same arbitrage is possible between the mini and big versions of the NASDAQ-100 contracts, NQ and ND, respectively. Mind you, the bigs don't trade all that much compared to the minis, but they do trade, and once you're set up to trade both contracts (many HFT firms are), it's no big deal to let your machines scan for this arbitrage after everyone else has gone home for the night.

Futures Versus Options

A more precise definition of the law of one price states that two securities and/or portfolios must be equivalently priced when they have the same future cash flows, or payoffs. Looking at securities this way, we can find arbitrage opportunities involving options.

Let's compare the payoffs of three securities we've already discussed: futures, call options, and put options. We'll use a fairly conventional diagram to examine these payoffs, which simply shows you the payoff of a security as a function of its delivery price (for futures) or strike price (for options) and of the price of the underlying instrument, or *spot price*, at the time of delivery (futures) or expiration (options).

In Figures 3.10 and 3.11 we see the simple, linear relationships between underlier price and payoff for a futures contract with a delivery price of 4. We ignore the effect of transaction costs and discounting entirely, although in practice those are obviously crucial considerations. (It might help to review how futures work in Chapter 2.) For the long position, when the spot price is 5, the payoff is 1. When the spot price is 3, the payoff is −1, indicating a loss on the position. And so on. For the short position, payoffs are exactly opposite, as you would expect.

Option payoffs are linear as with futures but have limited losses for long positions and limited gains for short positions. (See Figure 3.12.) For simplicity we disregard the effect of premium payments, which would push the "hockey sticks" up for short positions and down for longs. None of these option positions has a payoff like the futures, but see in Figure 3.13 what happens when we combine a long call and short put position into an option strategy known as a *synthetic futures* contract.

By combining a short put and long call into one portfolio, we have synthesized the payoff of a long futures contract. Now we have two portfolios with entirely different instruments but identical payoffs. The law of price says the value of these portfolios must be equivalent. As such, arbitrageurs can monitor both the real and synthetics futures markets looking for divergences, and sell the lower-priced and buy the higher-priced when they find them.

There are all sorts of arbitrage opportunities like this. Figure 3.14 illustrates relationships among stocks, indices, and derivative securities. Each of these relationships (indicated by an arrow) presents some of the potential arbitrage opportunity in the equity supermarket.

FIGURE 3.10

Long Futures Payoff

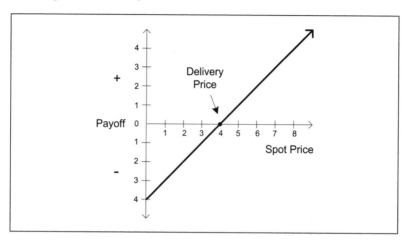

FIGURE 3.11

Short Futures Payoff

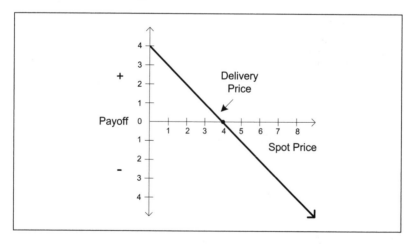

Options Arbitrage

We've touched on a handful of arbitrage strategies involving options, but there are a few other common ones worth noting. And note, too, that many arbitrage strategies for stocks

FIGURE 3.12

Option Payoff

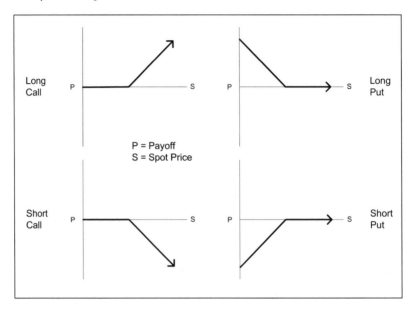

FIGURE 3.13

Long Synthetic Futures Payoff

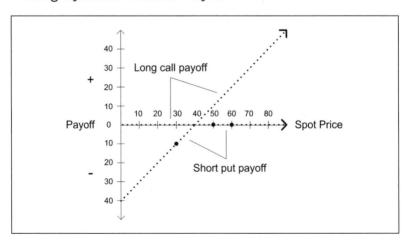

will work for options as well. For example, the cross-market arbitrage on two different exchanges—where the offer price

FIGURE 3.14

Arbitrage Opportunities

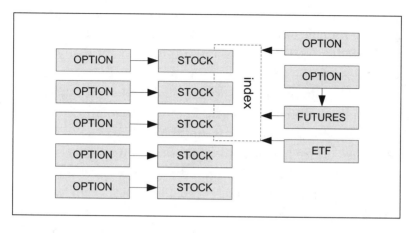

of a security on one exchange is less than the bid price of the security on another—generally works whether the security is a stock or option.

Volatility Arbitrage

The basic inputs to any option pricing formula are stock price, strike price, time to expiration, interest rates, and volatility. If the underlier is a dividend-paying stock, you also need expected dividend payments. The most interesting of these inputs, by far, is volatility. This is because volatility is the one input that cannot be observed. It is so crucial, however, that options traders assess the "price" of an option not only by its dollar price but by its volatility level. Although you can't observe it directly,[11] you can imply volatility given an option price and all the other input factors, and backing volatility out of the pricing calculation, generating an *implied*

---

[11] We mean you cannot observe volatility in real time, this instant. You can calculate historical volatilities, of course, by simply applying some math to a price history. But historical volatility is of limited value to the trader.

volatility (IV). Because you need an option price to imply volatility, this technique may not seem to be terribly helpful in calculating the price of an option in the first place (picture a recipe for chicken soup that calls for chicken soup as one of the ingredients). But it turns out it is quite helpful anyway. If you calculate the IVs of a sample of option contracts (different strikes, different expirations) you can then plot these levels on a three-dimensional grid known as a volatility surface. Figure 3.15 illustrates what it might look like.

The surface has time-to-expiration along one axis, strike price along another, and implied volatility level along the third. This gives you a fairly reliable indicator of what IV levels of any given option contract should be. Should you observe a contract whose IV does not lie on or near the surface, that contract is either overpriced (if the volatility is above the surface) or underpriced (if it is below). If it is overpriced, you sell it and buy a synthetic at the correct price. If it is underpriced, you do the reverse. That's something of a simplification, but the main point here is that volatility is one way to identify a mispriced option.

Spread Arbitrage

Earlier we saw the four basic payoffs of a position in a single option: long call, short call, long put, short put. While most options are traded as individual instruments, which result in one of these four payoffs, options can also be traded as sets of two or more different options in order to achieve some other payoff. These types of trades are known as *spreads* or *strategies*. Figure 3.16 shows an example of a very simple spread known as a *straddle*.

This spread consists of one long position in a call and another long position in a put, with both the call and put having the same expiration date and strike price. You can see the

FIGURE 3.15

Volatility Surface

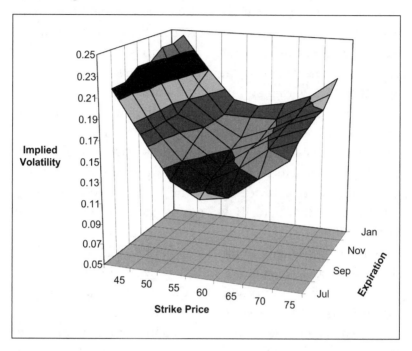

straddle has a positive payoff whether the stock price ends up quite a lot greater than or quite a lot less than the strike price. The holder of this spread is indifferent to whether the stock price increases or decreases and simply wants a substantial price change in either direction. For this reason, the straddle is an example of a direction-neutral strategy, or volatility spread, as the payoff is greater the more volatile the underlying stock (later on, we'll see an example of using the straddle to reduce exposure to volatility).

The price of a spread is simply the net price of the premia, or prices, of the component options, or legs. In Figure 3.16, the amounts by which the payoffs are vertically shifted down represent the premium. The call leg appears to have a premium of about $5, the put leg around $6, for a net premium of about

$11. In other words, should the underlying stock here end up with a price equal to K (the strike price), then the buyer of this straddle has lost $11. But if the stock ends up either above or below $11, the loss diminishes. And if the stock ends up far enough away from K—in either direction—then the straddle pays off. (If this were a diagram of a short straddle, the payoffs would all be inverted and vertically shifted up.)

Many spreads are so common (with names like *strangles*, *call spreads*, and *butterflies*) they are quoted and priced as if each was its own security even though each is really a set of multiple securities. As such, the larger option exchanges maintain separate order books for spreads. At the CBOE, for example, this book is known as the *complex order book*, or COB. If you want to buy the straddle presented in Figure 3.16, for example, you might see a market of 11.40 × 11.50 in the spread book. If you like this price, you can lift that offer, pay $11.50, and end up with a position consisting of one call leg and one put leg, as shown in Figure 3.16.

Clearly, the price of a spread is bound mathematically to the price of its legs; the former must equal the net of the lat-

FIGURE 3.16

Long Straddle

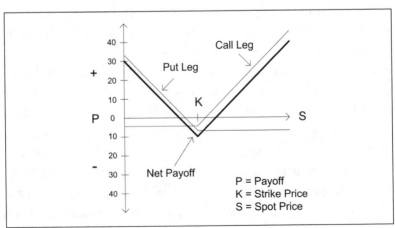

ter. If not, the law of price tells us there is an arbitrage opportunity. Going back to the example in Figure 3.16, we already
know we can buy the straddle in the spread book for $11.50.
If the order book for the call has a market of 5.20 × 5.25 and
the put has 6.20 × 6.25, then one can alternatively buy this
same exact spread (in the so-called natural market) for $11.50
($5.25 + $6.25), or the same price as in the spread book, by
submitting two orders: one to buy the call, one to buy the
put.[12] This is how the law of one price says things should
be. Now imagine the call market improves to 5.35 × 5.40 but
the put market remains 6.20 × 6.25 and the straddle market
remains 11.40 × 11.50. Can you see the arbitrage? If you are
fast enough, you can buy the straddle in the straddle book
for $11.50 and sell it back in the natural market for $11.55
($5.35 + $6.20) for an arbitrage profit of a nickel. Automated
spread arbitrage is a relatively new practice, as it requires an
electronic interface to spread books that exchanges have only
recently begun providing. And as more and more exchanges
follow suit, you can be sure more electronic arbitrageurs will
watch them like hawks.

PREDICTOR STRATEGIES

Our arbitrageur looks for cases wherein, at one particular
moment, some security is mispriced relative to some other
security (i.e., in violation of the law of one price). The aim of
our predictor—also known as a *quantitative trader* or *statistical
arbitrageur*—is to identify price discrepancies that involve a
time component. In essence, the predictor combs through mar-

---

[12] There is a risk, when trading a spread naturally, that you may get filled on
one leg order but not the other. This is known as *leg-in* risk. Many options
markets, however, allow you to specify a group of orders as a spread, and
they will only fill the combined order if all leg orders can be filled, thus
mitigating this risk.

ket data looking for cases where she can assert that a security trading at price Y will move over time to a higher price Z with enough certainty she is willing to buy at Y with plans to sell when it gets to Z. Or that it will move from Y down to X so she is willing to short it at Y and buy it back at X to close out the short. The length of the time component here can vary wildly. Because our interest is in high-frequency trading, we will focus on strategies intended to exploit changes expected to play out in at most seconds or minutes versus weeks or months.

Pairs Trading, Part 2

The pairs trading strategy shown earlier is, no doubt, the most basic example of a time-based mispricing with a time horizon on the short end of the spectrum. Here, one of a pair of stocks that typically move in concert with each other is identified as a laggard—it has not yet changed the way it is expected to, relative to the other. The predictor expects it to catch up (or down) with the leader eventually. But until it does, the predictor considers it mispriced. In statistical arbitrage terms, it is said to have, during this time period, *alpha*. Alpha is a measure of excess return, and it's widely used by predictors to quantify a mispricing. A vague assertion like "that stock is underpriced," no matter how true, does no good here. We need to know precisely, in pennies or fraction of pennies, exactly how much the stock is underpriced because we are delegating the actual work here to computers that require specific instructions. That's the job of alpha.

Once so-called alpha signals are detected (say, in a pairs laggard) and alpha is calculated, it is often expressed in terms of a *microprice*. This is the price the predictor is confident is the perfectly fair one, the price at which neither side of a trade will profit. For example, the microprice of MSFT may be, at some particular instant, $30.4971. Should it later be identified as a pairs laggard (say, to GOOG), its alpha might increase, bumping the microprice to something like $30.5112.

How is microprice used? Remember that all high-frequency trading opportunities are identified in one place and one place only: the order book. The predictor has her eyes—we'll call them her electronic eyes—focused on bids and offers as they change. She looks for bids that are too high and offers that are too low, according to her alpha strategy. She requires, of course, some price with which to compare those bids and offers to decide what bids to hit and what offers to lift. That price is the microprice, and it reduces the predictor's job at the order book to two basic rules. If a bid price is above the microprice, hit it. If an offer price is below the microprice, lift it.

There are likely to be other subtleties, such as how much a bid or price has to cross the microprice, and the predictor applies it not only when bids and offers change but also when her microprice changes. But still, compared with so much else in finance, this is one trivial task indeed. And this is the beauty of the microprice approach, the way it makes the electronic eyes' job—its algorithm—very simple. And simple algorithms are great because they allow the programmer to write extremely efficient code, code that can get the job done very quickly. Think again of algorithms as recipes. Which will take you longer to prepare: a fried egg sandwich or chef Charlie Trotter's chilled golden trout and California crayfish with citrus-cured salmon and sorrel?

Futures Lag

This strategy is not entirely unlike the arbitrager's futures versus basket strategy. In that case, however, we traded the entire basket against the index futures contract. Here, the predictor considers the component stocks individually, calculates an alpha for each based on its lag behind an index, and trades it accordingly. This strategy is also not unlike the simple pair strategy, but here a stock is not paired up with another stock but with a futures contract on an index in which the stock is a component.

Consider again the E-mini S&P futures contract (ES) traded at the Chicago Mercantile Exchange. This is a massively liquid contract, with something like $150 billion worth of contracts changing hands every day. Every day! That is roughly twice as much as the entire stock market. As such, the ES is considered by many to be the undeniable bellwether for the U.S. stock market. Its market, like many futures markets, is where "price discovery" is said to take place for the underlying cash market, which, in this case, is the combined market of the 500 largest stocks traded in the United States. In other words, when the investing community at large decides it is time to buy U.S. stocks—not some particular stock, but U.S. stocks in general—the trading starts here. For example, when some extraordinary news comes out with implications for the overall economy, the very first order book to reflect a change is more often than not the ES order book at the CME.

This might all seem quite backward, seeing that the S&P 500 index is supposed to reflect the average of 500 stock prices and not the other way around, but for reasons that go beyond the scope of this book, the predictor knows that market-wide price changes generally happen first in the ES, then in the component stocks. And because of the inconceivably huge amount of historical data available, the predictor can calculate for each of the 500 stocks a fairly reliable indicator of how exactly that stock price should change in response to a change in the ES market, for different stocks may have different sensitivities to the overall market.[13]

---

[13] The capital assets pricing model, or CAPM, refers to this sensitivity as a stock's *beta*.

For example, she may decide that for a 1 percent increase in the ES midprice under certain conditions (say, the increase occurs within one second), MSFT (Microsoft) should increase by 0.8 percent or 80 basis points. For a 1 percent decrease, MSFT should decrease by 80 basis points. And so on, for each of the 500 stocks. Now it's just a matter of watching the ES market for price changes, calculating a new microprice for each of the 500 stocks, and comparing those microprices against the order books at every market where that stock trades to look for opportunities. If a bid price is above the microprice, hit it. If an offer price is below the microprice, lift it. When the stock price adjusts, trade to get out of the position and take your profit.

How long does the predictor have to calculate all 500 microprices after an ES price change and get in front of the component stock changes? If she can't do it in a matter of microseconds—or millionths of a second—then she probably shouldn't bother trying. This is a well-known strategy, and firms have invested out the wazoo to get in on it.

This strategy can be used not only for lagging stocks but for other index futures. For example, by carefully analyzing market data, the predictor might discover a lead-lag relationship between the ES and the E-mini NASDAQ-100 futures contract (NQ), or perhaps the E-mini Dow futures contract (YM), and train her electronic eyes on those markets for alpha, just as she does the 500 component stocks.

Event-Driven

The basic idea here is to be the first to detect and react to events that are very likely—and many times certain—to affect the price of a security. Consider the unexpected announcement by a firm that they will cut their quarterly dividend, which hasn't changed from, say, 20 cents for several years, to 15 cents. Or that they have failed to meet quarterly earnings expectations, or that they have exceeded them, taking everyone by surprise. The surprise element here is crucial. If everyone expects a firm to cut their dividend or meet their earnings mark, those expectations will have already been reflected in market prices when the event actually occurs.

Barring insider trading, a surprise constitutes new and significant information that can be reasonably expected to move prices. For example, a dividend cut decreases the amount of future income you can expect from holding the stock and therefore depresses its value. If you were to short the stock the instant the announcement were made—before anyone else—you can expect the market price to fall. Once that happens, you can buy the stock to close out your short position at a profit. With an unexpected dividend increase, you would buy the stock and sell it after the rally.

Options market-makers must also keep a very close ear on dividend announcements, not just to take advantage of them but to avoid being run over. The calculation of an option price naturally must take into consideration the current price of the stock. For example, an option to buy at $10 when a stock is trading at $12 is at least twice as valuable as when the stock is trading at $11. That's easy to see. Now, a dividend payment can be seen as money "leaking" out of the stock.[14] An option to buy a stock that pays a dividend prior to expiration, then, will be worth less than if the stock did not. And the difference is based on the level of the dividend. If the level changes, so does the value of the option. Thus, if you are the first to respond to a dividend change, you can get in front of the expected price change in the options market just as in the stock market. And, if you are quoting that option, you will want to modify your quotes as soon as you possibly can, lest the event-driven traders pick you off.

---

[14] As my University of Chicago professor Ming Huang used to put it.

It's rare, of course, that a dividend or earnings announcement is a complete surprise to everyone. Analysts following a company very closely are likely to pick up on some of the same signals as the company's management and reasonably predict the announcement, even without the benefit of insider information. But even analysts are taken by surprise from time to time, and when they are, event-driven traders will race to get in front of the expected price adjustment before anyone else.

Trend Following

If you could accurately predict what stock prices will be, say, next week and have any interest whatsoever in making a lot of money, then you would be all set. Is a stock price going up? Buy it and get ready to sell it. Going down? Sell it short and get ready to buy it back. Nobody can do this, of course, and our predictor doesn't try to. She does, though, believe it is possible to identify trends over very, very brief periods of time. And she also knows she need not get it right all the time. If she can get it right just slightly more than half of the time and have the financial means to survive long periods of getting it wrong, then she is money ahead.

How, exactly, does the predictor recognize a trend? And how far out can she make a prediction? Sorry. Nobody doing this successfully is about to write a book about it—or to tell an author when he asks (trust me, this is true)—but there is at least one method that is said to have worked in the equity index futures markets. The idea is to monitor moving averages over different time horizons and compare the averages over shorter periods to averages over long periods. For example, every time a stock price changes, you recalculate two averages. One is the average of every price over the past five minutes. The other is the average of every price over the past five hours. If the five-minute average price is below the five-hour average price, the market is said to be trending down. If the opposite is the case, it is said to be trending up. Perfect? Of course not. But again, you need only be right more times than you are not.

Other trend-following strategies—also known as *momentum* strategies—might borrow from the field of fluid dynamics, or other branches of the physical sciences, to fit observed price changes to a model that can then be used proactively to identify trends as they occur with some reasonable degree of certainty. As with many things in nature (weather changes, water flowing from a spigot, and so on), it's not difficult to look at a price chart of, say, the S&P 500 and draw some basic and reasonable—if not infallible—conclusions. For example, stock prices generally don't jump instantly from one price to another, distant price. A stock might certainly change from $5.00 to $30.00, but it's not going to do so in one tick. It's going to follow a path—maybe a short one, but a path nonetheless—just as, say, the weather is not going to change instantly from downpour to sunshine.

Something else you might notice is that price increases tend to follow other price increases, and decreases follow other decreases. This doesn't happen all the time of course, but your analysis just might convince you that it happens a good amount, perhaps even a tiny majority of the time. Scientists have fit natural observations to reasonably predictive models for ages, models that are refined and improved over time and never quite perfect. The predictor can, and does, apply the same thinking here. Not that it's easy. It's excruciatingly difficult to identify tradable trends that are something better than wild gambles, especially with so many firms now searching for the same thing. But it doesn't stop firms from trying and, occasionally, succeeding.

Mean Reversion

We've already seen how the phenomenon of price dynamics due to supply and demand imbalances has influenced the investor and market-maker, and it turns out it's quite a meaningful thing to the predictor as well. An increase on the bid side of an order book is going to push the market up, roughly in proportion to the relative size of the increase. An increase on the offer side does the same thing in the other direction, pushing prices down, again in some relation to the size of the increase. The imbalance response doesn't go on forever, of course. It peters out. It does, though, appear to generally go too far, and then bounce back, as it were. In other words, markets tend to overreact to imbalances then correct themselves. Prices are said to revert to the mean, or, roughly, the midprice of the market. They may not revert entirely, of course, especially, say, if there is repeated pressure on the same side of the market. But there have been more than enough observations of this so-called *mean reversion* to make it statistically significant and, therefore, something of great interest to our predictor.

Think again of the 500 ⎢1.00 × 1.10 ⎢500 market that gets a visit on the bid from the 5,000-lot elephant. The market might shoot up to something like 1.15 × 1.20 before the elephant gets its fill, but the predictor knows these are ephemeral prices. This market has alpha when it peaks; say the predictor calculates a microprice of $1.10. She's going to hit those $1.15 bids like mad, shorting all she can at that price. When the market reverts to its mean, say the original 1.00 × 1.10, she'll be only too happy to lift those $1.10 offers, buying back the shares to close out her short position, making a nice clean nickel for her efforts. And knowing the elephant may have more to buy, she won't waste any time closing the short before the beast comes back. Mind you, this is an extreme example with prices plucked out of the air, but it illustrates the basic idea.

THE ASCENT OF THE HIGH-FREQUENCY TRADER

Earlier, we described the high-frequency trader as a selective market-maker who uses superior execution speed and prediction capabilities to earn trading profits. For example, it's not uncommon to find high-frequency traders using an alpha-based microprice as the baseline for their bids and offers, then leaning those markets based on their inventory. The alphas may be derived from trend following, mean reversion, pairs trading, or some other predictive strategy. Trend following is particularly appealing. Consider a 1.04 × 1.05 market and a high-frequency trader confident in a downward trend to, say, 1.00 × 1.01. He can certainly do something like hit the $1.04 bid, wait for the market to trend down to 1.02 × 1.03, and lift the offer to close out the short and make a one-penny profit. Knowing the trend isn't over, he can do the same thing again, hitting the $1.02 bid and waiting for the offer to trend to a lower price or at least an equivalent one, in which case he can scratch for the rebate.

Although general interest in the high-frequency trader came on like a supernova in the wound-licking early months of 2009, he didn't appear suddenly. He evolved from the traditional market-maker over the course of several years, an evolution attributable at least in part to two important trends.

The first trend involved the adoption of computers, by more and more buy-side firms, for working large orders. There was a time when an institutional investor, such as the broker for a mutual fund manager, could call around on the telephone and privately "show" a large order to several pro-spective market-makers, each of whom he knew personally, confident those traders would not get in front of the order. Why so confident? Because those traders had reputations to maintain. If a sell-side trader were to get a show call from a broker, say, "No thanks," and then hang up and make a trade that moved the market away from the broker, that trader was unlikely to get another show. His livelihood was at stake and he knew it. But as more and more brokers began using com-puters to work their orders, the reputational risk all but van-ished. If a market-maker could detect signs of an iceberg, for example, and tow it to his advantage, who would ever know? As other firms likewise learned the pattern recognition tech-niques to smoke out hidden liquidity, the game shifted from how to detect liquidity to how to do it faster than the next guy. Automated liquidity detection became fair game and the computational arms race was on.

The second trend helping to explain the emergence of the high-frequency trader from the ranks of the traditional market-maker stems from a phenomenon known as *adverse selection*. The idea here is that when information and/or capabilities among market participants is asymmetric—that is, some people know more than others or have better skills than others—the market tends to favor the more knowl-edgeable and/or capable. One way this plays out in the securities markets is the so-called "well-informed trader" problem. Consider the market-maker, up against a better informed trader out there. The other trader may have new insights based on careful and tedious analysis of earn-ings or management plans or something along those lines, insights the market-maker doesn't have. Or the other trader may be a quantitative trader—our predictor—who performs bleeding-edge statistical analysis on screaming-fast comput-ing hardware. This predictor can make reasonably confident predictions based on very strong alpha signals, thereby seeing something in the markets that others do not, or at least before they do. The conventional market-maker, full of blissful ignorance, might be making a 1.00 × 1.02 market when the better informed trader knows the stock is worth, say, $1.03.

You get the idea. Is a market-maker going to stand for this very long? Of course not. And when spreads narrow to a penny or less, it's that much easier for a small informational advantage by the well-informed trader to become a costly disadvantage to the less-informed market-maker. Bottom line, in the most actively traded stocks, the market-maker can only expect to make profitable markets by getting just as smart as the predictor. If you can't beat 'em, join 'em.

CHAPTER 4

Achieving Speed

The most brilliant high-frequency trading strategy won't do you much good until you implement it, and you'd better do a good job. A poorly built HFT system is worse than no HFT system at all. Worse for you, that is. The firms with optimized and battle-tested systems already in place—the sharks who already swim these waters—are only too happy to see new little fishes show up. They taste good.

In this chapter, we'll touch on some of the strategies not for trading but for actualizing trading strategies through the design and implementation of a custom software and hardware solution, or HFT system. This is the collection of computer servers running the software that, in a nutshell, listens to market data in search of profitable trading opportunities, which it then attempts to realize before somebody else does. In Chapter 5, we'll walk through a sketch of a hypothetical HFT system, or take a look under the hood, if you will.

This focus here on technology is not to diminish the importance of trading strategy, to which we've already devoted a fair amount of ink. Profitable trading is the reason for its existence, right? Nor is our emphasis on technology meant to in any way diminish what you might consider the third leg of the HFT milking stool, the one you can find one hundred twenty degrees from each of the trading and technology legs. I refer to mathematics. The folks who toil over the math behind an HFT system are *quantitative analysts*. If you get the math wrong in this game you are just dead. And there is a mountain of it. Quantitative analysts deal with relatively simple things like calculating present values of expected dividend streams and the proper recalculation of option prices after stock splits and mergers, and more daunting things like maximizing the efficiency of multidimensional correlation matrices and choosing from among various forms of finite difference methods for pricing options, all while sipping coffee from a mug as likely as not to be decorated with the Black-Scholes partial differential equation—which they know by heart.[1]

While we're on the topic of human talent, it should go without saying that the absolutely, positively, most important determinant of the success or failure of an HFT operation is the team of men and women assembled for its planning and implementation. If the true secret to success

---

[1] And so can you. One form of the Black-Scholes partial differential equation (PDE) looks like this: $\frac{\delta f}{\delta t} + rS\frac{\delta f}{\delta S} + \frac{1}{2}\sigma^2 S^2 \frac{\delta^2 f}{\delta^2 S^2} = rf$. According to Black, Scholes, and Merton, this equation must hold true for a derivative on an underlying stock (given certain assumptions, e.g., that the volatility of the underlying stock is a constant—which as it turns out is definitely not true, but we shan't go farther down that path in this slender text). This is not, by the way, the Black-Scholes option pricing formula. One gets that by establishing a boundary condition on the price of an option and backing out a formula for an option whose price satisfies the PDE. The key variables in there are f for the price of the derivative, t for time, S for the price of the underlying stock, σ for volatility, and r for the risk-free interest rate. The terms on the left are partial derivatives. For example, the first one denotes the ratio between an instantaneous change in f (i.e., over an infinitesimal stretch of time) and an instantaneous change in t. The rest is just, well, math.

in HFT—as in countless other complex endeavors—were printed on a bumper sticker, it would certainly read, "It's the People, Stupid." The best operations out there are the result of a nearly serendipitous uniting of just the right talent and personalities and motivations required to pull off the daunting task of building a successful HFT operation. The key individuals are imaginative, driven, forward-thinking people with just enough ego—but not so much that they can't get along with other such driven, forward-thinking people with healthy egos. And success here goes beyond hiring rock star traders, developers, and quantitative analysts. Rock stars are an asset, no doubt, but their roadies and managers had better be just as impressive. A scant few examples: Software must be tested, and testing or QA (quality assurance) in an HFT shop can be grueling due to relentless time pressures and system complexity; not everyone can do that well. Network engineering is an art and craft all its own these days; it's no wonder that individuals with credentials such as the Cisco Certified Architect can practically name their salary in this field. And note, too, that most of the emphasis in this book is on the so-called front office of the trading operation, which encompasses everything up to the moment of a trade. Once a trade is done, key back-office operations such as clearing, compliance, and margining come into play. These are hugely important jobs, invaluable in their own right.

You might already notice a presumption that in order to compete effectively in HFT, a firm must build its own, customized HFT system. Why? There are packaged software solutions one can license for high-frequency trading. In the options space, for example, reputable firms such as ORC, Actant, and RTS provide automated market-making software with all of the features you might need—quoting engines, electronic eyes, auto hedgers, and so on. Some firms have no doubt had success using these products (otherwise, one can presume, the vendors would not have survived). The firms at the forefront of HFT, however, will tend not to rely on third-party software but rather to build their own. Building your own system is certainly more costly, perhaps by orders of magnitude. But the firm willing to make this investment can enjoy distinct advantages over those who do not, for two chief reasons.

BUY OR BUILD?

When using the very same tools as your competition, your advantage is limited to how you use those tools. And this is not an insignificant point. Two drivers, for example, given turns on a track with the very same Ferrari will no doubt demonstrate different abilities. When you build your own tools, however, you can gain advantage from the quality of the design and workmanship that goes into them. For example, as we'll note later, the efficiency of one's HFT software algorithms is highly variable depending on who is coding the software. Some programmers are better than others. For all intents and purposes, there simply *is* no driver when an HFT system is racing around the track. The design and construction of the system is where you prove yourself better than the competition.

Another reason HFT firms will choose to build, when they can, is more prosaic. It allows them to modify their software whenever they choose to. Third-party software vendors will forever entertain your requests for modifications and bug fixes, but with more than one customer to please, the vendor must queue and prioritize such requests. The most aggressive HFT firm will simply not tolerate having to wait, say, for the next product upgrade from the vendor. They want to fix bugs and add enhancements on their own timetable, and this is only possible when you build your own. Anyone who has worked in trading system development (even before HFT came around) knows that ad hoc "patches" or "EBFs" (emergency bug fixes) between scheduled releases are a fact of life.

It is possible, of course, to take the must-build-our-own mind-set too far. The wise HFT firm will choose to build some components—but not all. For example, there is little advantage to building components some would term infrastructural. A database is a good example of something belonging to infrastructure. So, too, are the messaging components, which we'll discuss presently.

Combining Products

We've already seen how the arbitrageur exploits the pricing relationships among different securities and/or portfolios of securities. It behooves the HFT system designer to consider these relationships when maximizing the efficiency of strategy implementations. The opportunities are particularly abundant in the options space. Consider these contracts:

- **SPX**—Traded exclusively at the CBOE, the underlier of this European-style[2] option is the current level of the S&P 500 stock index. The SPX is a cash option

---

[2] A European-style option may only be exercised on its specified expiration date. An American-style option may be exercised at any time up to and including the expiration date. All other factors equal, American options are worth more than the European. And if you are wondering, the distinction has nothing to do with geography. Although someone clearly had geography in mind when they came up with Bermuda-style options, which may be exercised on any of a set number of days up to and including expiration. The value of a Bermudan option, then, is somewhere between that of a corresponding American or European, just as Bermuda is located between Europe and the United States.

that settles (when the option expires in the money[3])
according to the difference between the index level
and strike price upon expiration.

- **XSP**—Known as the mini SPX and also traded at
  the CBOE, the underlier of this European-style cash
  option is one-tenth the value of the S&P 500 index.

- **ESO**—Traded at the CME, the underlier of this
  American-style option is one E-mini S&P 500 futures
  contract, or ES. If an ESO expires in the money (e.g., a
  call option with exercise price below the current ES),
  its holder receives a position in the ES.

- **SPY**—The underlier of this American-style option,
  which today trades at all U.S. exchanges, is the Spider
  ETF or tracking stock. This option, when it expires in
  the money, settles into shares of the ETF.

The commonality of these four contracts is, of course, the
derivation of their value from the S&P 500 stock index.
Holding everything else constant, when the index moves, so
do the theoretical values of each of these contracts. And there
are plenty more S&P-dependent option contracts than just
these. The values of the different contracts in the S&P complex move differently, of course, depending on the structure
of the contract. For example, the XSP is based on one-tenth of
the index, whereas the SPX is based on the full index level.
And the style of an option (American versus European) must
be taken into account. But those are mathematical details,
comparatively easy for the quants to sort out.

---

[3] At any time of its life, the "moneyness" of an option reflects the difference
between its strike price and the current price of the underlier. A call option
whose strike price is below the current underlier price is said to be *in the
money*. When the strike price exceeds the underlier, it is *out of the money*.
And when the strike price is approximately equal to the spot price of its
underlier, it is said to be *at the money*.

How can one take advantage of this commonality? One obvious way is by sharing a volatility surface. Figure 3.15 shows a data structure that maintains a potentially unique volatility level for every combination of strike price and expiration date. In addition to the current price of the underlier, the current volatility level of the index is one of the most crucial inputs when pricing an option. Clearly, then, you need only maintain one S&P 500 volatility surface and use it to drive the pricing of each of these contracts.

Beyond just pricing, the commonality of contracts in the S&P options complex can be particularly powerful in risk management. As mentioned earlier, for example, an options market-maker doesn't always have the opportunity to lay off the risk of an option trade with another trade in the same contract. The most difficult risk to lay off is vega, or the sensitivity of an option price to changes in underlying volatility. Just as with the calculation of theoretical prices, the calculation of option sensitivities (Greeks) such as vega also takes volatility as an input. The bottom line here is that by maintaining a common volatility surface for all these related products, one can maintain a single vega for the entire complex, and therefore lay off vega risk in one product by trading the other. For example, if you *sell vol* by writing an SPX call or put option, you can *buy vol* to offset it by purchasing, say, SPY options.

DESIGNING FOR CHANGE

The best high-frequency trading strategist knows the half-life of any given strategy is not terribly long, that trading strategies must evolve and be replaced. This same forethought can be applied when designing HFT systems. As any software engineer knows, some designs lend themselves to extensibility, as it's known, and some do not. Two concepts most engineers strive for here are modularity and loose coupling. *Modularity* simply means that a large system is comprised of smaller components or modules built more or less independently (although certainly designed with one another in mind) then connected together to form a larger working system. *Coupling* refers to how system modules interact, or communicate with one another. If these lines of communication are simple and minimal, the components are said to be loosely coupled. On the other extreme is tight coupling, in which two or more components require relatively complicated messaging and are otherwise highly dependent on one another. The goal here is a confederation of highly independent components, or *objects*, which hide their internal doings or implementations behind simple interfaces. Systems of loosely coupled components are comparatively easy to change because to add new functionality, you simply create and introduce new objects. Such architectures also tend to be superior for their resilience against breakage when the system is changed.

The ideal (utopian?) goal here is a system in which you can introduce a change to one component, or repair a component, or add an entirely new component, with little or no adverse effect in some other component. The opposite is a system so fragile, whose internal interdependencies are so complex as to be practically unknowable, that some innocuous bug fix can bring the whole thing down. You don't want a system like this any more than you'd want a car whose brakes stop working when you replace a headlamp.

Modularity and loose coupling are software system design concepts, but there are also things one can do when managing the development process in order to facilitate the creation of systems designed for change. The term of art here is *methodology*, but anyone caught actually using that word is likely to be run out of the shop before they get the third syllable out of their mouth. It is terribly easy to go overboard here, to replace common sense with ideology and ceremony, and software developers with a few years under their belts will know what I mean.

Still, there are some methods—er, practices—that most people agree are pretty good. Most of them center on the concept of evolutionary, or incremental and iterative, development as opposed to "big bang" approaches, in which a massive system is designed entirely and in great detail before anything is built. The idea here is to start with an overall system sketch, if you will. You always need some vision of the big picture, the ultimate goal, even before you begin. But you'll be much happier to use an erasable whiteboard marker than, say, permanent ink. Once a tentative design is up on the board, you start to build, ideally with the most difficult or high-risk components. You build a small number of these, get them into a running state, and then assess with honesty and humility what works and what doesn't. Then you go back and modify them, adding functionality and new components once what you've got is running pretty smoothly. The philosophy here, oft repeated and borrowed ultimately from Mother Nature, is that complex systems that work tend to evolve from simpler systems that work.

When striving for architectures of loosely coupled objects, and software development processes that facilitate the evolution of great software, it is, of course, possible to reach too far. Indeed, because the concepts of modularity and incremental development are really so obvious as to be self-evident, the real trick is to recall the old saw about not letting perfection become the enemy of the good. At the end of the day, we have paychecks to cut and bills to pay, and investors or shareholders to please, and systems that remain forever trapped on a whiteboard are unlikely to help. It's impossible to say how one can know for sure when an architecture or development process is good enough. That comes from experience, and even with experience you can never be quite certain. When I worked at Bank of America, despite the amazing talent of the traders and developers building their fixed income derivative pricing systems, we would still remind each other of the need to just "get stuff done" on a fairly regular basis. As such, we needed only say or write the initials "GSD" in order to remind everyone of the need to produce good software—and not just great ideas.[4]

DISTRIBUTION AND LOAD BALANCING

So now we've got this picture in our heads of an HFT system comprised of a slew of independent components, each doing its own thing and doing it well. One component will listen and republish market data ticks. Another will look for alpha. Another will submit a trade order. And so on. The system has been componentized, you might say, or *distributed*, to use the software engineering term of art. But to how many components should work be distributed? Do you delegate some whopper of a task to ten different components, or twenty? The trick here is to modularize enough such that no module is overly bogged down, as doing so defeats the purpose of modularization, but not so much that the intermodule messaging burden doesn't grow so large that it bogs down your messaging mechanism, about which we'll say more in just a bit.

The distribution we've talked about so far is functional (i.e., the decomposition of a large task into a series of smaller tasks). Another related concern of any HFT system designer is how to balance computational loads when there is a lot of the same kind of work to be done. Consider the need for calculating the microprice of each of your stocks. You may

---

[4] We didn't use the word *stuff*.

very well decide to have a single component that does nothing but take in X number of input factors, do a bit of complex mathematics, and return a single microprice as an output. With, say, 3,000 stocks to price, you must decide how many of these components you will instantiate, each of them working in parallel with one another. Certainly you won't want to have just one, as this would invariably lead to a processing queue, or backlog, and you don't want that. Nor, however, are you likely to want 3,000 of these devices. Any one of them is likely to spend more time idle than actually working, and the overhead of this many instantiations is likely to bog down machine resources such as the computer's processor and memory. With a modest amount of experimentation, you can decide the right number.

Machine allocation is yet another aspect of the distribution and load balancing dilemma. A given server can handle only so many processes before it gets bogged down (again, memory and processor) and workloads back up. Once you've decided how to modularize functional components, and how many of each instance is required, the final job is to allocate those processes across a given number of servers. Again, with planning and experimentation you can arrive at the right allocation.

The end game here is not unlike the planner of hamburger stands at a stadium. For a given transaction, there is an order to be taken, buns to be filled with meat and fillings, french fries to be made and bagged, drinks to fill, supplies to be fetched from storage areas, etc. To have one employee do all of this is inadequate, but you certainly don't need a separate person to do each of those tasks. That's the functional decomposition. Next you must decide how many cash registers, how many grills, how many potato fryers, and so on. That's load balancing. Finally you'll decide how many of these stands to put around the stadium. With just one, the lines will back up, and some customers will need to walk so far they won't bother. With too many, the overhead cost will force you to charge more money than customers are willing to pay.

INSANELY EFFICIENT SOFTWARE

When a programmer writes software to perform some task, she will choose some algorithm or another before actually writing code, making her selection based on some criteria or another. The smartest HFT programmer, or developer, will always make algorithmic efficiency one of the most crucial of these criteria. And she will devote endless time to making her algorithms more and more efficient. The more efficient they are, the less time they require to do their thing, and as we know, time really (*really*) is money in HFT.

An algorithm is an approach to solving a problem. It's not so much a set of instructions, because that implies the instructions are in some tangible form. The algorithm is more abstract than that; it's the idea behind the instructions. And for any given problem, there are likely to be many, many possible solution algorithms. Consider the problem of finding a given entry in a phone book, which everyone knows contains names sorted alphabetically. To retrieve a number, we first must find the name, and there are different ways we might go about this.

Say we are looking for Sara Gruen. One way is to start at the first page and flip forward until we find "Gruen, Sara," but this approach, while perfectly effective in finding the name, is also unnecessarily slow—an intuitively inefficient use of our time. Another approach, one we may use instinctively, is to start by making a guess and opening to a page based on the first letter of the last name. In this case, we might open the phone book not quite midway. Say we land on "Mortenson, Greg." Knowing that Gruen comes alphabetically before Mortenson, we will go *halfway back* to the beginning and find ourselves at, say, "Eggers, Dave." Knowing Gruen comes after Eggers, we go *halfway forward* toward Mortenson and find ourselves at, say, "Lamott, Anne." Then halfway back again toward Eggers, and so on in such a manner, until we find ourselves at "Gruen, Sara," where we then find her phone number so we can give her a call.[5] Computer scientists label this approach a *binary search algorithm*, and it is indeed far more efficient than the *linear search* we first contemplated.

HFT developers do, in fact, find themselves having to choose from among various searching and sorting algorithms, of which there a great many, each with different characteristics with respect to things such as time efficiency, space efficiency (memory required), and accuracy. But they also find themselves toiling over designs for the very most efficient algorithms for problems very specific to high-frequency trading. For example, consider the developer who is charged with writing code for the modification of option quotes in response to a change in the underlier price for a given symbol,[6] say, SPY. There are nearly 2,000 option contracts on the SPY, each with a different expiration and strike and type (call/put) and each with its own order book. The options market-maker, then, might have upward of 2,000 bids and 2,000 offers in the market at any given time. Should the underlying ETF market price change,[7] ticking up, say, by

---

[5] To tell her how much we liked her book *Water for Elephants*.

[6] An option "symbol" here refers to the stock underlying an option.

[7] The ETF is not the only possible underlier to monitor for pricing SPY options. One can also drive the pricing of these options using the E-mini S&P futures contract (ES) because the ultimate underlier for these options is the S&P 500 index, which is, of course, the source of both ES and SPY prices.

a penny or two, the market-maker may need to update every one of those 4,000 prices as quickly as possible. This entails sending the exchange a long series of update requests, each of them instructing the exchange to replace a quote for exactly one contract.

Here, not only will the developer choose the most time-efficient algorithm for getting those requests out the door, but she will also consider which of the thousands of contracts to begin with. Does she begin with the nearest-term, lowest-strike contract and proceed in order with the next listed contract, proceeding through the list in a linear fashion until all contracts are updated? Or does she begin with the most actively traded contracts? Or does she begin with the deepest in-the-money contracts (calls with low strikes, puts with high strikes), knowing that these contracts have the highest delta sensitivities and are therefore more subject to hedging risk should they trade? Or does she choose some other algorithm? There is no perfect algorithm here, but the inventive and persistent developer will, with a bit of analysis and experimentation, arrive at what seems the best quote update procedure.

The efficiency of a given program is subject not only to the choice of algorithm by the programmer and the quality of her programs, but also by the choice of programming language in which they are written. This is the set of English-like code (writing software is also known as *coding*) with which the programmer types her instructions using keywords and symbols according to strict semantic and syntactical rules, to be compiled and linked so that her instructions are ultimately in binary form (ones and zeros), which is the only instruction language a computer ultimately can understand. There are three predominant languages used in the development of software for trading systems. C++ (pronounced "C plus

plus") is an object-oriented[8] extension of the C programming language and derives much of its power by its "closeness to the machine." With C++, a programmer can write excruciatingly specific instructions, allowing her to fine-tune instructions in her quest for ultimate software efficiency. C# ("C sharp") and Java are also quite popular, also object-oriented, although not as expressive as C++, but easier to program.

All other factors equal, a programmer is likely to write a program in C# or Java faster than she can with C++, and the program is less likely to contain errors. There are two notable drawbacks of C# and Java, however, when it comes to HFT. First, as mentioned, C++ allows the programmer to be more specific in her instructions than do those languages. This enables her to do things like refer to specific locations in memory (using *pointers* and even *pointers to pointers*) and even manipulate individual bits of memory. C# and Java don't allow the programmer to get quite so close to the machine, which isn't necessarily bad because the opportunities for introducing bugs are greater with C++ than with C# or Java by quite a substantial degree. But it does limit the specificity with which the programmer can write programs. The second drawback has to do with memory management, in particular the releasing of memory once a program is done with it, a chore known as *garbage collection*.

---

[8] The venerable C programming language is geared toward so-called *procedural programming* in which functional instructions (do this, do that) can be kept well separated from the data on which functions are performed (do *it* to this, do it *to* that). C++ supports so-called *object-oriented programming* by allowing one to bind function and data together into constructs known as objects. An object (an instantiation of a *class*) encapsulates or hides its data parts and functional parts, or *implementation*, behind a well-defined *interface*. Object orientation is appealing for its facilitation of extensibility (i.e., modifying programs to do new things) and robustness (i.e., reducing the opportunity for bugs by hiding the code inside an object from other code).

One of the appeals of C# and Java is that they take care of this collecting of garbage for the programmer, noticing when memory is no longer needed and making it available for more work. With C++, the programmer must generally write specific code to keep track of memory she is using and release it when she's done with it. If not, her program will place a lock, if you will, on some area of memory, memory thereafter unavailable to other programs even when her program is done executing. (Such bugs are known as *memory leaks*.) The problem with automatic garbage collection is that you may have little or no control over when it will happen, and the garbage man might show up at very inopportune times. For example, your electronic eye may notice a particularly juicy trading opportunity and attempt to submit an IOC order to take it out, only to find itself in a holding pattern while garbage collection takes place. This kind of indeterminism can make the difference between getting a trade or not. For reasons such as these, C++ is generally the language of choice for writing HFT system components requiring the greatest efficiency and determinism. C# and Java remain very popular, and quite appropriate, for less time-critical components of the system (e.g., GUI apps[9] and report generators).

It so happens that even your choice of operating system can have an impact on the efficiency and determinism of your software. Most HFT systems run on a standard Linux or Windows[10] operating system. Now the job of an operating system is massive. It has far more to do than run any given

---

[9] GUI app = graphical user interface application.

[10] Don't even get me started on the Windows versus Linux debate. They are both fine operating systems with their respective strengths and weaknesses, and at the end of the day, choosing one or the other may have no appreciable difference. But don't try to tell that to the more ideological inhabitants of the software development community.

program, and it has plenty of housekeeping chores that most programmers don't even know exist. The end result is that even writing the most efficient C++ program possible will not guarantee that the computer will perform a task precisely when you want it to. Again, executions are for all intents and purposes indeterministic. There are, however, operating systems that do indeed allow you to know precisely when the computer will do something for you. These are known as real-time operating systems (most are variations of Linux), and given the need for efficiency and determinism, they are considered very seriously by the most demanding and sophisticated HFT firm.

The body of code behind an HFT system is massive, consisting of hundreds of thousands or even millions of lines of code (more if C++, fewer if C# or Java). Each line of code is an opportunity for strengthening or weakening the system. And each line of code is one step in an algorithm, of which there can be tens of thousands, each of them an opportunity for improving the efficiency of the overall system or gumming it up. It's no wonder HFT developers work very, very long hours. (They get paid well, too.)

AWESOME MESSAGING

There's another important aspect to the architecture of a system of distributed components, one the HFT designer takes very seriously, and that is how components will communicate with one another. This is sometimes known as the system's messaging infrastructure as the data passed between components are know as *messages*. Messages are also sometimes know as *events*, and systems like our HFT system are hence known as having *event-driven* architectures. There is no clear beginning or end of the work with a system like this.

Components are started up and just sit there, basically, until something happens—some event—and they react in some way or another, triggering events that other components respond to, and so on.

One very popular approach to messaging is based on the concepts of publication and subscription, or *pub-sub*. Here, components are designated as publishers of messages, subscribers of messages, or both. For example, a market data component may be responsible for publishing ticks as they arrive from an external source. Another component, say a pricing engine, may be a subscriber to ticks. To make sense of this, there is typically some sort of catalog of message types, sometimes known as *tags* or *topics*, and components sign up, as it were, for either publishing or subscribing. (A single component will generally not both publish and subscribe the same tag.)

An obvious analogy here is the magazine. Firms publish various titles, and households subscribe to titles of interest, and as new issues of magazines are published they are dutifully delivered to their subscribers. (And a firm that publishes a magazine may also subscribe to other magazines to keep an eye on the competition.) Another analogy comes from the field of microbiology, where different cells secrete different chemicals and whatnot through their membranes, which also only permit certain chemicals to come in. This lets cells sit awash in whatever other cells are emitting but only take in what they care about. That's pretty much what goes on inside a system with pub-sub messaging, as illustrated in Figure 4.1, where some messages are allowed into a component and some are not.

While the pub-sub model is very widely accepted and practiced, there are different ways to go about actually implementing it. And here, by the way, we find a decent example of an element of an HFT system for which a number of very

FIGURE 4.1

Messaging

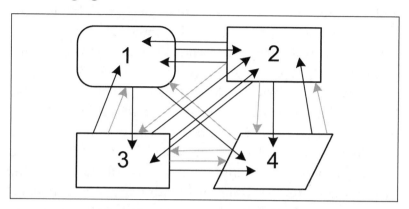

good solutions are available from third-party software providers. Some HFT firms will no doubt always want to build their own pub-sub infrastructure, but some very successful firms do quite nicely by letting vendors take care of this crucial bit of, er, plumbing. The first example likely to come to the minds of anyone in this business is the Rendezvous product sold by the software firm Tibco. This venerable product has been around for many years, and I don't think I'd be too far off the mark to say that more than half of all HFT firms have "a Tib" at the heart of their system. Tibco does not have a monopoly, however, and newer firms such as 29West and Tervela (which we'll discuss again) are giving the good folks at Tibco a good run for their money.

Another choice in the area of messaging is how messages should actually move from one component to another. One approach is to have two components establish a direct, unbroken connection with each other using something known as *TCP/IP sockets*. It's not unlike having a direct phone line with someone, a line that is always open and used exclusively by you and the other party. This exclusivity is one reason (of several) a socket connection is considered among the most reliable means of communication between two components. But it is an inherently "one-to-one" solution, and with hundreds or thousands of components needing lines of communication, it can be dreadfully unwieldy to use sockets for every possible pair of components needing to communicate with each other.

A popular alternative to sockets is known as *multicast*. Here, a publisher broadcasts messages across a network with no particular subscriber in mind. It just emits messages like a radio antenna and lets the subscriber worry about getting them. If a component is interested in subscribing to a multicast message, it must listen for it with its receiving antenna (and network routers must be configured so the multicast messages get to the receiver in the first place). Multicast is very practical for getting messages to massive numbers of subscribers; however, multicast is traditionally an unreliable means of transport.[11] There is no guarantee that a given message will reach its subscriber, as there is with most TCP/IP socket transports, just as there is no guarantee a regular phone call will go through the first time you try to place it. TCP/IP sockets and multicast aren't the only possible transport mechanisms out there, and the HFT system architect will spend a fair amount of time choosing just the right messaging approach from among the various alternatives.

PROCESSING OFF THE CORE

There's an interesting thing going on with the evolution of computing—a devolution of sorts—having to do with the actual place in a computer where computation, or processing, takes place. When we talk about a computer in the modern sense, we're really referring to a machine with two features

---

[11] There are, nowadays, reliable multicast protocols.

that sets it apart from earlier computational devices, features that one could argue are the very reasons for the explosive growth of computing since the mid-twentieth century. One of these is the concept of a stored program, whereby instructions are not hardwired into physical circuitry but kept on some external medium—punch cards and paper tape in the early days, magnetic disks and flash memory these days—to be read by the computer when it was time to get some work done. The other is the concept of a general purpose computer, embodied by a central processing unit (CPU) capable of executing not just one type of computational task but virtually any task whose instructions could be expressed in and read from a stored program. And as everyone who has ever bought a computer knows, the power of available processors grows every year. The Intel 486 was king for a time, until the Pentiums came along, which have now of course been dethroned by Xeons and whatnot. It's impossible to keep up with the march of progress, and the computer manufacturers seem to like it that way just fine, so long as we keep replacing our PCs every other year or so.

The whole key to building the next gotta-have-it computer is figuring out how to pack yet more power into that processor, that general-purpose programmable brain that can do anything you ask it to. There are some users of computers, however, who have used their own brains to arrive at a notion that seems utterly wrong at first, an idea that seems as sensible as going the wrong way on an escalator. Is it really necessary or even wise, they ask, to pack all of the computing work on that one little chunk of silicon? If you only need a computer chip to do one thing, is it necessary to have one designed to do any number of different things? Can't we delegate at least some of the processing to a place in the computer other than one of the cores of a CPU? Aren't there some computing applications—say, high-frequency trading—for which this approach might make a lot of sense? The answer to that last one appears to be yes.

One example of such "processing off the core" is in an aspect of computing of which any user of a networked computer—which is to say, virtually any user—is happily ignorant. If you doubt this, ask the next dozen or so non-programmers you know, "How do you like the TCP/IP stack on your Windows laptop?" and see how many don't look at you funny. "You know, the WinSock!" you might continue, if you're speaking to someone whose opinion of your sanity doesn't much matter. Imagine the task of moving some small product, say office supplies, across the country. Imagine each type of supply—stapler, eraser, pen, whatever—is in its own box with a label on it. Imagine those boxes are loaded into small trucks. Imagine those small trucks are themselves loaded onto large trailers. Imagine those trailers ride atop flatbed rail cars. Now imagine the train has arrived at your station and you want to get to the number 2 pencils.[12] First you have to identify the right train car, then the right vehicle carrier, then the right truck, then the right box, then remove your pencils. And if you want to send pencils back, someone needs to put it in the right box, the right truck, and so on.

While the analogy is imperfect (a better one might go the other way and have the pencils split into molecules and then atoms), this sort of layered transport mechanism is not unlike the way data moves around the network. And something at each node must do the packing and unpacking. That something is typically the CPU. Roughly speaking, whenever a new packet arrives, the CPU must pause whatever else it is doing to open up the packet and move its contents

---

[12] Author's son: "Hey, Dad. If number 2 pencils are so popular, why aren't they called number 1?" Author: "You make that up or steal it?" Author's son: "Stole it." Author: "Figured."

into memory where it can be accessed by programs. And when a packet needs to go back onto the network, the CPU is again interrupted to move it out of memory and onto the network.

It's exhausting! Wouldn't it be nice if something else could take care of this? Enter the *TCP/IP offload engine*, or TOE. The TOE card, as it's often known, takes care of moving data between the network and memory, freeing up the CPU to do other things. Because virtually every computer is forever moving data off of and onto a network, this can take quite a load off the processor, thus allowing it to devote more cycles to tasks like identifying trading opportunities, submitting orders to exploit them, and so on.

Any number of computing functions traditionally done on a CPU are potential candidates for moving off the core. The TMX Message Switch offered by the already mentioned Tervela, for example, provides an entire pub-sub messaging bus implemented in hardware. It works much like a software-based pub-sub, with components publishing and/or subscribing to data of interest to them, but the actual provisioning and storage of data is done not in memory but in the physical circuitry of hardware. The throughput of the TMX is wickedly impressive. It does, however, place an intermediary between message publisher and subscriber. As such, some engineers debate whether or not the inherent latency or "bump" of any intermediary—no matter how fast—can make a hardware-based message switch more efficient than a direct software connection. Still, the TMX is taken seriously by an impressive coterie of HFT firms and is a prime example of the devolution of general-purpose computing.

Another example of moving processing off the core— and this is even more radical than TOE cards and hardware message switches—involves moving work from the CPU not just to a specialized device, but to a specialized device repurposed for general-purpose computing. That device is the GPU, or *graphical processing unit*, and the concept here is known as GPGPU, or *general-purpose computing on a graphical processing unit*. The original intent of the GPU, interestingly, was to offload computer graphics processing work from the CPU. Just like the shuttling of data between a network and memory, the elemental task in graphics processing is rather simple—determining the color and intensity of a single pixel on the computer screen, essentially—but there is just a ton of it to be done. The GPU came about to take care of this specialized task so the CPU wouldn't have to. With GPGPU, the GPU takes care of tasks having nothing whatsoever to do with graphics processing.

Now for sure, a GPU cannot perform the complex computational tasks that a CPU can. But it can perform simple tasks, and it can perform a gazillion of them all at once, or in parallel. As such, there are plenty of computational tasks in HFT that are not good candidates for GPGPU. But some of the work behind HFT is just perfectly suited for it. One such job is the pricing of an option using a method known as Monte Carlo simulation (MCS). The value of an option, as we know, is derived primarily from the price of its underlying security, such as a stock, which is presumed to move through time on a more-or-less random path.[13] Using MCS, one generates, or models, a huge number of possible price paths; figures the option value for each one; and then takes the average to arrive at a reasonable estimate of the current value of the option. The calculation of a random price path for a stock turns out to be a relatively simple task: Start with some price, then add or subtract some random amount to get to the next price, and repeat ad nauseam. This is easy stuff for GPGPU.

---

[13] The path follows geometric Brownian motion, to be precise.

PARALLEL PROCESSING

With GPGPU, we saw how a big problem (calculating an option price) can be solved by breaking it into a large number of smaller taks and executing them simultaneously. Such parallel processing is not limited to the exploitation of GPGPU. We saw it before, in fact, in our discussion of distribution and load balancing, where the HFT designer determines how many of a particular component to replicate on a given machine and how many machines running the same components is optimal. There are also opportunities for parallel processing on a single CPU. A quad-core processor, for example, is very much like four processors bundled together. It allows the programmer to write code in which up to four tasks can be performed simultaneously. A GPGPU can perform not just four tasks in parallel, but hundreds or perhaps thousands. But CPU manufacturers are, of course, not going to stop at quad-core, eight-core, or even sixteen-core processors. It's not inconceivable to imagine CPUs with hundreds of cores in the foreseeable future, allowing parallel processing right there.

DIRECT ACCESS FOR MARKET DATA AND EXECUTION

The HFT firm requires low-latency access to an exchange for two fundamental tasks. One is the receipt of market data, the other the submission of orders or quotes, also known as trade execution. Any delays here will naturally slow things down, so the most aggressive firm will obtain this access by the most direct means possible.

Market data consists mostly of changes to an order book (new bids, new offers), notifications when trades are executed (someone's bid matched someone's offer), and the current state of a market (closed, opened, halted, etc.). Depending on the type of security, one can obtain market data directly from an exchange or by way of a consolidator. Market data for virtually all stock markets, for example, is provided by the Consolidated Tape Authority, or CTA, which is now part of NYSE Euronext, which provides two feeds. Order book changes are disseminated via the Consolidated Quotation System (CQS) feed, and trades via the Consolidated Trade System (CTS) feed. Participating markets stream real-time data to the CTA, which consolidates it and sends it out directly to recipients or to market data vendors who resell it to their customers.

Most stock markets also provide market data directly. Options market data is also available in both consolidated and direct form. The consolidated version is provided by the Options Reporting Authority, or OPRA,[14] which includes quotes, trades, and market states from each of the subscribing exchanges.[15] Futures market data is provided directly by the Chicago Mercantile Exchange and the Intercontinental Exchange.[16]

The most aggressive HFT firm will have a direct market data feed from every exchange on which they trade, in addition to CTS/CQS and OPRA, and they will shun third-party resellers in favor of getting the data directly so as to avoid

---

[14] It appears that exactly half of all people in the industry pronounce the acronym "OPRA" like the first name of Ms. Winfrey. The other half pronounce it like the musical/theatrical art form made popular by Rossini, Wagner, Mozart, et al.

[15] As of June 2010, these are CBOE, ISE, NYSE Arca, NYSE Amex, NASDAQ Options Market, NASDAQ PHLX, BOX, and BATS.

[16] Much of this market data is disseminated by way of the Secure Financial Transaction Infrastruture, or SFTI (pronounced "safety"), a highly reliable and low-latency computing network dedicated to market data. Like the CTA and OPRA, it is owned and managed by NYSE Technologies.

the delay naturally introduced by an intermediary.[17] You might wonder why anyone would bother getting market data from a consolidator rather than directly from each exchange. Naturally, the latter approach is more costly due to the need to maintain not one connection (to a consolidator) but several connections to several exchanges. Cost is no object for some of the larger HFT firms, yet still they will listen to consolidated feeds. For one, no market data feed is perfect. Having multiple sources of data helps one, for example, to verify that an unusual market data tick is real and not an error by having a second source to compare it to. Also, it is possible in some cases to get a price change on a consolidated feed sooner than from a direct feed. This has to do with how the exchange disseminates its price changes. In general, an exchange will immediately post a price change to, say, OPRA. But it may use a polling strategy for disseminating to direct subscribers, publishing new ticks at some interval, say, every 500 microseconds. Should a price change happen right after the polling interval, OPRA subscribers will get the tick before direct subscribers.

When accessing an exchange for trade execution, the HFT firm has a choice similar to that with market data. Every exchange will allow a firm to submit orders directly via, for example, a dedicated data circuit. As well, many broker-dealers will also accept orders from their customers that they in turn relay to an exchange.[18] As you would expect, the HFT firm wishing to reduce latency here will choose to submit orders and quotes directly, bypassing any intermediary.[19]

---

[17] They might, however, and very wisely, license software developed by a firm that specializes in market data handling but instantiate that software in their own data centers.

[18] The Goldman Sachs REDI offering is widely used for this purpose.

[19] This path into an exchange gives rise to a controversial practice known as naked access, which we'll cover when we get to benefits and risks of HFT.

NATIVE APIs

Once a firm decides to interact directly with an exchange, bypassing any intermediary, there is another important choice to be made. There are basically two alternatives here. One is to use an industry-standard messaging format—for receiving market data, submitting orders, listening for responses, etc.— known as *FIX*, short for *Financial Information eXchange Protocol*. The other is to write code in a way that the exchange's computers can interpret directly, by using the native *application programming interface*, or *API*, specific to that exchange.

The advantage of FIX is obvious. No matter what exchange you are communicating with, you write your instructions in exactly the same way. (We are talking here, by the way, about very, very specific coding considerations that only a programmer need worry about: Do I place the trade price in the fourth field of the array or the fifth? Where do I specify what contract I want to trade? And so on.) That universality saves the firm a bundle of software development dollars. When writing to native APIs, the programmer must literally start from scratch when the firm wants to interact with a new exchange. It can easily take weeks or even months to plan, design, code, and test a program that uses a native interface.

Why, then, would anyone not use FIX? It has to do with translation time. When an exchange receives a message in its native format, no translation is generally required. The HFT order, for example, is processed immediately. When an exchange receives a message in FIX, the message must be translated from FIX into the native format, then processed. We're not talking about a lot of time—well under a millisecond in most cases. Still, the most aggressive HFT firms will gladly make the investment in software development to get their orders in that much faster.

Some exchanges, it should be noted, do not allow access via native APIs. They may provide market data only in FIX,[20] or receive orders only in FIX. In these cases, since nobody has an advantage, the HFT firm will happily use FIX.

COLOCATION

One of the stones no HFT firm will leave unturned in their quest for lowest possible latency is the physical location of their HFT system servers relative to the location of the exchange-matching engines. All else equal, the firm with closest proximity to an exchange market data server or matching engine will have an obvious advantage over everyone else. Consider two firms, A and B, each watching a 1.00 × 1.10 market on NYSE Arca, each ready to lift the offer should it improve to $1.09. The electronic eye of firm A is housed in Carteret, New Jersey, in the same building as the NASDAQ matching engine. The electronic eye of firm B is in a data center in Newark, New Jersey. Say that scenario happens, with someone offering 500 shares at $1.09. Each firm fires its order at the exact same instant (assuming they get the market data tick simultaneously). Firm A's order arrives and gets the fill. Firm B's order arrives 300 microseconds later. They get nothing. Nobody wants to be firm B in this scenario. As such, the practice of *colocation* has become all but *de rigueur* in the world of high-frequency trading.

Each of the stock, options, and futures exchanges has exactly one, primary matching engine (see list in Table 4.1). That engine is located in a data center either owned by the exchange or leased from a colocation facility provider (for example, Equinix in Secaucus, New Jersey, or Savvis in

---

[20] A newer variant of FIX, known as Fast FIX, is particularly popular for the dissemination of market data from exchanges.

Weehawken, New Jersey). The colocating firm simply leases rack space, installs its servers right there, and uses a *cross-connect* network link to connect its servers to the matching engine gateway servers. You might rent just a single "2U" space in a rack that is big enough to slide in one server roughly the dimensions of a large pizza box, or you might rent an entire cage of racks, or even multiple cages. These servers are connected, of course, not only to the exchange-matching engine but to other servers in the HFT system, and ultimately to the firm's trading desk so traders can monitor what the system is doing. The larger HFT firms, then, will house their HFT system not in one location but in several locations across a WAN, or *wide area network*. The firm trading on the big four stock markets and all options and futures exchanges will have locations at each of the facilities shown in Table 4.1.

How much of a difference does colocation actually make? For the Chicago firm that is trading on New York exchanges (and vice versa), colocating in New York will save 12 to 15 milliseconds, which is roughly how long it takes for data to move between those cities, due primarily to the speed of light in glass. Within the New York area, it takes roughly 300 to 500 microseconds to get packets from one of the major colocation sites to another. In addition to physical distance, the directness of a circuit can also make an appreciable distance. A network connection from point A to point B is rarely comprised of just a single, unbroken fiber. It may be comprised of multiple fiber links, each connected by a router or switch, in the same way that a route from one end of a city to another is going to consist not of one straight shot but several legs connecting at intersections. Each intersection or "hop" in a network is an opportunity for an additional few microseconds of latency.

TABLE 4.1

Exchange-Matching Engine Locations

Exchange	Matching Engine
Stock	
BATS	Weehawken, NJ
Direct Edge	Jersey City, NJ (2010: Secaucus, NJ)
NASDAQ	Carteret, NJ
NYSE	Weehawken, NJ (2010: Mahwah, NJ)
Options	
BATS Options	Weehawken, NJ
Boston Options Exchange (BOX)	Newark, NJ
Chicago Board Options Exchange (CBOE)	Chicago, IL
CBOE C2 (2010)	Secaucus, NJ
Chicago Mercantile Exchange (CME)	Chicago, IL
Intercontinental Exchange (ICE)	Chicago, IL
International Securities Exchange (ISE)	Jersey City (2010: Secaucus, NJ)
NASDAQ Options Market	Carteret, NJ
NASDAQ PHLX	Carteret, NJ
NYSE AMEX	Weehawken, NJ (2010: Mahwah, NJ)
NYSE Arca	Weehawken, NJ (2010: Mahwah, NJ)
Futures	
Chicago Mercantile Exchange (CME)	Chicago, IL
Intercontinental Exchange (ICE)	Chicago, IL

CONNECTIVITY EXPRESSWAYS

The aggressive HFT firms will colocate in each of the U.S. matching engine locations, distributing their HFT system across these half dozen or so sites in order to minimize communication latencies with each exchange. But there's a rub. Because the same products (or highly correlated products) trade at multiple exchanges, it is crucial that the sites act in concert with one another. For example, if the firm's electronic eyes in Weehawken take out a massive bid on some stock at the NYSE such that it wants to lean its markets on the offer-side to complete the round-trip, the electronic eyes in Carteret need to receive these instructions as quickly as possible; otherwise it might itself take out bids on the same stock on NASDAQ, growing its position more than it wants to. It would be like sending out a team of travelling salesmen, back in the days of Willy Loman, and having them unwittingly sell more product than the company actually has due to their inability to communicate with one another quickly enough.

In a perfect HFT system, then, each site would communicate with the others instantly, as soon as it made a trade. This is literally impossible, of course, due to that stubborn law about the speed of light. Still, it is possible—for a price— to connect the HFT system sites such that intersite communication is minimized. High-frequency trading firms, then, devote a good deal of thought and planning to the building of their so-called WAN.

The ideal high-frequency trading WAN will have its sites interconnected by sufficient *bandwidth* such that messages can pass from one site to another as quickly as the laws of physics will allow. Bandwidth is a measure of how many units of data (typically a bit) can move through a network segment in a given unit of time (typically a second). For example, a 1 Mbps segment will move, on average, one million bits per second. A 1 Gbps segment will allow one billion bits per second. These days, the aggressive HFT firm will connect sites with circuits in the tens or hundreds of Mbps range, depending on how many securities it trades.[21] The

---

[21] These days = early 2010.

so-called "sizing" of a circuit, wherein a network engineer determines the appropriate bandwidth between two sites, is not an easy task. It's difficult because data doesn't move at a steady stream between colocation sites. It tends to "burst" at random intervals depending on the market activity, and estimating the sizes and durations of these bursts involves a fair amount of educated guessing and experimentation. Getting this wrong on the high-side, say, by putting gig bandwidth everywhere, can be extraordinarily costly even for the most well-heeled HFT firm. Getting this wrong on the low-side leads to traffic jams of data.

Imagine a stretch of small highway that can easily accommodate a "bandwidth" of 100 cars per minute. Imagine a basketball arena on that highway when a game is letting out, and 500 cars all want to use that highway at the same time. They'll get through eventually, but not as quickly as if the highway were sized for 500 cars per second. The same thing happens with HFT when a burst exceeds the bandwidth. The messages all jam up and wait. With highways and basketball arenas, occasional backups may be acceptable. In HFT, it can lead to the possibility of one site not getting messages, say, to change their markets when they need to.

There are a variety of choices when it comes to connecting your colocation sites, ranging in cost. At the lower end is a *virtual private network* or VPN, sometimes called *tunneling*. Here, your data actually moves across the public Internet (for at least part of the journey) but in specially protected packets. It's as if you hired a secure moving company to pack your stuff in unmarked, armored trucks before driving it to your new home on public highways. Your stuff is protected, but still subject to delays if traffic gets heavy.

One very appealing means of low-latency data communication for the high-frequency trading WAN is the SFTI network. Owned and operated by NYSE Technologies, you might think of SFTI as a giant loop of outrageously high-bandwidth fiber, wending its way in and out of major cities, not unlike the U.S. interstate highway system.[22] Now picture every stock, futures, and options exchange has an ultrahigh-bandwidth circuit connecting their matching engines and market data publishers to the SFTI ring. Now, if you are an HFT firm wishing to connect to any of those exchanges, you too need only to make a connection onto SFTI using one of the many "on-ramps" provided for just such purposes. You'll still pay for the bandwidth and exchange connections that you actually use, but it's a heckuva convenient way to get your WAN up and running.

Another way you might implement your WAN is by using one of several so-called *extranets* owned and operated by private data communication providers. Here, the provider constructs its own private network of "highways" connecting various points, and you pay the provider for permission to move your data on it. You are still sharing those highways, but the extranet owner keeps track of how many vehicles are on the road at one time and can therefore reasonably guarantee bandwidth.

At the far end of the cost spectrum are private, dedicated circuits that you—and only you—can use. You might have to pay a fortune for it but can be certain the road will be clear when you need it. If you are in the league of paying for dedicated, high-bandwidth circuits, you still will make your choices here carefully. Two providers, for example, may advertise seemingly equivalent circuits, but one of them may take a more circuitous route than the other, introducing more hops and therefore opportunities for delay.

---

[22] There are actually two such "loops," each carrying the same data in the event one of them goes down.

REAL-TIME MONITORING

There's one more aspect of building an HFT system that might seem like a yeah-whatever but can really mess you up if you don't get it right. HFT systems are inherently intricate due to the sheer complexity of the job they are try- ing to do. Multiple exchanges, thousands of products with varying degrees of price correlation, cutthroat competition, intricate regulatory restrictions—the list goes on. The better your system can monitor itself and provide the information to humans they need to oversee it, the better off you'll be. Even a modest-sized HFT system will consist of thousands of different component processes (programs, basically) run- ning simultaneously at different sites and all directly or indi- rectly affecting one another. The humans on the desk, both the traders and the system support staff, must have tangible assurance that everything is running properly. And when things go wrong—which they do, all the time—the humans need to know as quickly as possible what happened, and what's being done or needs to be done to address it. There is little worse than to see your system do a bad trade—sell for too little or buy for too much—and not know what happened.

Ironically, the problem in situations like this is not too little information but too much. In many cases, each of the thousands of running processes is continuously writing to a log file when things happen (e.g., receive tick from market data publisher, send request for discount rate, receive dis- count rate, calculate theoretical price, etc.). These log files get massive before you know it. Ultimately, the information you need to diagnose a problem is in these log files, somewhere. But this does no good to the trader who is reduced to lob- bing F bombs when the system does a bushel of bad trades. Having to wait for a developer to find the right log, read it, think about it, discuss it with other developers—you get the picture. No good. There are all sorts of ways the HFT system designer can accommodate such real-time monitoring, and no one way is absolutely better than another. But one way or another, it's gotta be there.

This discussion of implementation strategies is not a definitive one, of course. The creative and competitive minds working at HFT firms will—by necessity—dream up new strategies for getting a leg up on the competition. But it gives a fair idea of the thinking that goes on in this important corner of the HFT universe. Now let's examine a hypothetical HFT system that employs some of these strategies.

CHAPTER 5[1]

Under the Hood

Now let's open up the hood of a hypothetical HFT system and see what's under there. The system described here is not based on any actual system but should give you some idea of what real ones might actually look like, as well as an appreciation for their complexity. As you would expect, detailed plans for actual HFT systems—blueprints, if you will—are closely guarded secrets of the firms who build them.

Our system is designed to support the implementation of just about any of the strategies we've discussed. As such, it will trade all products across our U.S. equity supermarket—stocks, options, and index futures—and further demonstrate how tightly interconnected those markets are. We'll interact with both equity futures exchanges, all options exchanges, and the top four stock exchanges: NYSE, NASDAQ, Direct Edge, and BATS. Expanding the sketch to include displayed ATSs would not be a big deal.[1]

---

[1] Expanding to dark pools is also conceptually simple; however, their lack of displayed markets would require some modification to the logic behind our quoting engines and electronic eyes.

This is a front-office system, responsible for pricing, trading, and risk management. We won't get into the back-office tasks such as clearing, margining, accounting, and other such functions. Those are supremely important elements of any trading operation, no doubt, but they are generally insensitive to the speed of trading and hence out of our scope.

Our sketch assumes we've already secured rights for direct access to raw market data from each exchange, as well as rights to trade directly on each exchange. We use no broker-dealers or other intermediaries between us and the exchange-matching engine. Each exchange provides access rights in a slightly different way. Some still require an actual membership in the exchange (such as the CBOE, although this is about to change as these words are written), and others simply charge a monthly fee for whatever it is you want to do, letting you choose as from a menu. We also assume we are well up-to-speed on the rules and regulations with which we must comply at each exchange and have completed any necessary qualifications, such as trader examinations. Finally, we also assume we have an arrangement with a clearing firm that will ultimately take responsibility for the finalization of our trades at the end of each day and with which we have posted necessary margin funds, or have taken the necessary steps to become a self-clearing firm.

HFT SERVER SITES

Our first view of the system is a geographical one, indicating the physical locations of computer servers. These are housed in data centers at eight sites. Six are colocation sites for low-latency access to exchange-matching engines and market data publishers, and two are control sites for coordinating the actions of servers at the exchange or remote sites. The control sites also include trading and support desks where humans monitor and maintain the system as needed.

The reason we place servers at the exchange sites is, of course, to minimize market data and execution latencies. When the exchange publishes a tick, we want to receive it as soon as possible; we also want to receive consolidated ticks, via CTA/OPRA, as soon as possible, so we'll also colocate at their source. When we submit an order or quote, we want the exchange to receive it as soon as possible. The total number of exchanges we wish to interact with is fifteen. Fortunately, some of these house their matching engines at the same data centers, where we can lease colocation space for our HFT system servers, so the number of required exchange sites is only six. Table 5.1 shows a list of the remote sites, what we care about at each, and what types of product trade at each exchange.[2]

Figure 5.1 shows the WAN on which our system does its thing, implemented using an extranet, as described earlier. We might also use SFTI for some or all of our WAN. We might also use a dedicated circuit for each of the nodes on the graph; it would just cost more. The main thing is that any site can communicate with any other site. Note the WAN includes two control sites, one each in Chicago and New Jersey, for the servers that coordinate the activities of the remote sites and for the human traders and support staff. Also note the lack of any intermediaries between our system and the exchanges. Market data will come in directly from the exchange and not via any third party.

---

[2] This snapshot of colocation sites and primary matching engine locations is accurate as of March 2010. There is a bit of uncertainty, e.g., when the CBOE will launch C2, but this information is otherwise fairly reliable as to what's where.

TABLE 5.1

Colocation Sites

Site	Address	Matching Engine/ Market Data Source	Products
Carteret	Verizon 1400 Federal Boulevard Carteret, NJ	NASDAQ Stock Market	Stocks
		NASDAQ Options Market	Options
		NASDAQ PHLX Options	Options
Chicago Lakeside	Equinix 350 Cermak Boulevard Chicago, IL	Chicago Mercantile Exchange (CME)	Futures, futures options (S&P 500, NASDAQ 100, Eurodollar)
		Intercontinental Exchange (ICE)	Futures, futures options (Russell 2000)
Chicago Loop	CBOE 400 S. LaSalle Street Chicago, IL	Chicago Board Options Exchange (CBOE)	Options
Mahwah[1]	NYSE Technologies MacArthur Boulevard Mahwah, NJ	NYSE Stocks	Stocks
		NYSE AMEX Options	Options
		NYSE Arca Options	Options
		CTA/OPRA (market data)	Stocks/options consolidated
Secaucus	Equinix 755 Secaucus Rd Secaucus, NJ	International Securities Exchange (ISE)	Options
		Boston Options Exchange (BOX)[2]	Options
		Direct Edge	Stocks
		Chicago Board Options Exchange (C2)	Options
Weehawken	800 Harbour Boulevard Weehawken, NJ	BATS Stock	Stocks
		BATS Options	Options

[1] NYSE is planning to open the Mahwah facility in late 2010. Until then, everything listed here for Mahwah is located at the Weehawken site.

[2] As of this writing in March 2010, the BOX is located at the Level 3 facility at 165 Halsey Street in Newark, NJ. They recently announced their plans to relocate to Secaucus.

FIGURE 5.1

Server Sites

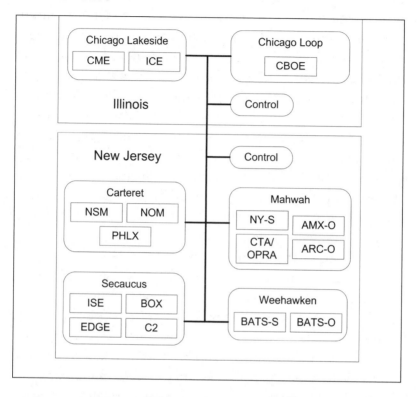

INFRASTRUCTURE: MESSAGING AND DATABASE

As we'll see presently, the work of our system will ultimately be carried out by a confederation of loosely coupled software components. In order for these things to talk with one another, we'll place a Tervela TMX Message Switch and supporting products at each of our remote and control sites. The TMX will act as a relay between any components needing to communicate with one another.[3]

---

[3] Tervela, you will recall, implements a pub-sub messaging system in hardware. For a software-based solution, we might choose the equally impressive LBM and associated products from 29West.

To set up the TMX, and this is true for any pub-sub type messaging solution, we'll need to define a set of topics, or message types, that components will use when communicating amongst themselves. For example, one topic might be designated "Trade" and be used whenever a component wishes to announce to the rest of the system that a trade has occurred. The Trade topic will include a strictly defined set of details, such as what product was traded, the exchange, the trade price, and so on. Any component caring about trades will subscribe to this topic. The topic list for a typical HFT system can get positively massive and include thousands of different topics for things like changes in a theoretical price, receipt of new market data ticks, human trader changes to system parameters, and on and on.

Like most any computer system, an HFT system will generate all manner of data that needs to be stored. Records of tradable securities (e.g., stock symbols), trades, positions, end-of-day prices, exchange IDs and passwords, trader names, and on and on—all of this must be permanently stored for all manner of purposes. For one, when the system or any of its components is restarted (either intentionally or due to a crash of some sort) it must know the state of things— current positions, human-set parameters, and so on. And, of course, this data will be mined for queries and reports. Our system will include a relational database at each site, such as Sybase or Oracle, for this purpose.

COMPONENTS

We're ready now to address the software programs, or components, that carry out the actual business of high-frequency trading. If the network, messaging, and database infrastructures provide a stage and lighting, the components are the actors performing the play. These actors will be written in C++ and run on a custom distribution of the Linux operating system, optimized to remove anything we don't need,[4] and installed on servers with multicore processors. These loosely coupled and highly autonomous components will communicate with one another using the aforementioned TMX and use the database for permanently storing and retrieving data as needed.

We'll do a few things to goose up the performance of our components. For one, we'll use TOE[5] cards to relieve the processors of responsibility for moving data on and off the network, leaving more cycles for our HFT components. And, of course, we'll want to take advantage of parallel processing capabilities of our multicore servers, distributing the components' work across however many cores there are. Doing so requires that components programs be written as multithreaded, which is a comparatively daunting effort for programmers or, at the least, a lot more involved than single-threaded programming. Fortunately, Intel provides the C++ runtime library Threading Building Blocks, or TBB, to take care of all these pesky details, so we'll use that and save many, many hours of development time (and headaches).

The componenture of a typical HFT system can be massive. It's not uncommon for a large-scale system to consist of thousands of instances of component software programs running simultaneously, all interacting with one another to do the work of high-frequency trading. These systems tend to be highly complex. But as with most complex systems, many components play similar if not identical roles, so it is not terribly difficult to organize its components into types of component.[6] We can organize the components comprising

---

[4] This is not unlike a racing shop stripping down a stock car to only what's needed for racing.

[5] TOE = TCP offload engines, as discussed earlier.

[6] In a pure object-oriented system design, these types might be considered high-level *classes*, from which will derive inherited subclasses, *instances* of which would comprise the executable system.

our system, for example, into five different types: Thinkers, Listeners, Pricers, Traders, and Managers. Figure 5.2 shows how they interact.

The components we call *Thinkers* take direction from humans and convert it into instructions for other components. For example, different HFT firms will, of course, attempt different strategies. One may trade only stocks and deploy strategies such as rebate scratching or slow-mover takeout, while another stock-only firm may attempt to move elephants and follow trends. Another firm may trade stocks, options, and futures and attempt more challenging strategies such as volatility arbitrage. The system we are sketching here will indeed encompass the high-frequency trading of stocks, options, and futures and can thus be used for virtually any of the strategies discussed thus far. In addition to strategy implementation, our Thinker components will also take care of simpler tasks, such as managing the set of tradable securities, again according to what the humans decide to trade.

FIGURE 5.2

Component Interaction

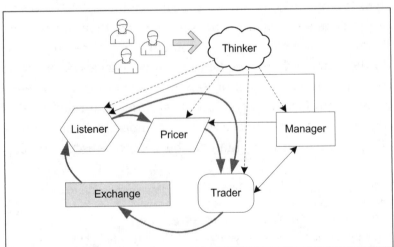

With hundreds of thousands of tradable securities—five thousand or so stocks, three hundred thousand or so option contracts—this bit of housekeeping turns out to be a task not to be taken lightly.

The *Listener* components take in market data and make it available to other components. They sit as close as possible to market data sources—exchanges and CTA/OPRA—and take in every tick. They check it for errors, arbitrate when multiple sources disagree, and republish it for the rest of the system. And they do it all very, very quickly.

Pricer components do what you might guess. They calculate, in real time, the prices of all securities. These are the prices that Trader components will use when looking for trading opportunities. As such, they are biased according to both alpha and inventory. Pricers receive instructions for detecting alpha from Thinker components and instructions for inventory biasing from Managers.

Like Listeners, *Trader* components interact directly with exchanges but for the purpose of submitting orders and quotes. They receive market data ticks from Listeners, trading instructions from Thinkers, and theoretical values from Pricers. They report their trades to Managers.

The essential work of *Manager* components is to control the work of other components, principally the Traders, based on trading activity and other meaningful events. For example, as trades occur, the Managers maintain position data for each security, which is communicated back to Pricers for inventory biasing. Managers are also responsible for the crucial task of telling Trader components to modify or cease their trading in response to high-risk events such as bad trades.

Notice how Listeners, Pricers, Traders, and the exchange are connected by a directional, somewhat circular set of interactions. This is the crucial *low-latency loop* of any HFT system. A tick comes in from the exchange, the Listener checks it out and dashes it off, Pricers use it to reprice, and Traders use the new price to get trade orders to the exchange. The faster that all can happen, the more competitive we will be. As such, when implementing our HFT system, we will take advantage of any technological or logical optimization we can think of to shave milliseconds and microseconds out of this loop wherever we can. Other interactions, such as between Thinkers and Pricers, are less sensitive to latency considerations.

What follows is a rundown of the key components in each of our categories. Except where noted, instances of these components run at each of the remote sites. This is not an entirely complete list, and any actual system is likely to include all manner of proprietary components, but these are all the generic ones. And the descriptions of component functions focus on essential business considerations. Some particularly mind-numbing details are omitted. Once we've summarized what each of these components does, we'll step through a scenario to demonstrate how they interact to do the actual work of high-frequency trading.

Thinker Components

The components responsible for taking direction from humans and converting it into instructions for other components are the Strategy Server, Securities Manager, and Compliance Manager.

Strategy Server

As you'll see soon enough, most of the components are highly specialized and do really just one thing. The essential purpose of the Strategy Server is to take direction from humans (traders, quants, support) and turn it into specific instructions for the other components, based on what strategies those humans wish to attempt. For example, a firm wishing to implement the futures lag strategy would use the Strategy Server to instruct the Stock Pricer component to calculate alpha for each component stock of the index underlying the futures upon a change in the futures price. It will also, when components start up, provide them with configuration information so they know exactly how to behave that day. The Strategy Server is in this way rather analogous to the morning meeting you'll find in conventional, floor-based (non-HFT) firms, where risk managers and traders gather before the markets open to set strategy and trading limits for the day.

An important design consideration with respect to the Strategy Server is to consolidate this intelligence in one place rather than spread it out in this place and that so it is comparatively easier to maintain. If the instructions, say, for the trend-following strategy, were scattered all over the place and you wished to modify the implementation of the strategy, you'd have to make your change in multiple places and would be more likely to miss something. The communication of instructions from the Strategy Server to other components is not time-critical, so we need these only at the control sites.

Securities Manager

The job of this component might seem relatively unsophisticated but is very important nonetheless. It keeps track of all securities the system will trade. In essence, it keeps a list of stocks, futures contracts, and option contracts and pertinent details about each one. For stocks, these details include such things as a schedule of expected dividend payments and earnings announcements. For options, details include data like expiration date and strike price. Futures contracts and stocks can be manually entered by humans. Because there are so many option contracts, however, these are best handled automatically.

New option contracts are listed nearly every day. For example, say Acme Explosives is trading around $50 and the highest available strike price for a call option is $80. If Acme's stock price climbs to $60, exchanges are likely to add a new option contract with a strike of $90. Most new contracts are listed overnight, so the Securities Manager will run jobs at the end of the day or very early in the morning to pick these up from the Options Clearing Corporation (OCC)[7] and/or individual options exchanges. It will also query those sources intraday for strikes added during the trading day. We need a Securities Manager only at the control sites.

Compliance Manager

Compliance! Ah, this is the joy of any trading shop, the compliance with rules governing the trading of securities. Many of those rules have to do with the filing of reports, the qualifications of traders, and other such matters of no concern to the HFT system designer. Some rules, however, apply to the moment-by-moment operation of an HFT operation. Compliance with those rules must be built right into the system.

One example is the so-called "legal width" rules of options market-makers at certain exchanges. These rules place a restriction on a market-maker's bid-ask spread, or width. Most options exchanges, for example, require a width of no greater than five dollars during most of the trading day, which is such a gargantuan spread as to be meaningless in many cases. Legal widths are much narrower, however, for the first few moments of the trading day and vary according to the bid price and expiration date of the option. The Compliance Manager maintains the details of all rules like

---

[7] The OCC is owned collectively by the options exchanges and is principally responsible for the clearing and settlement of option trades.

this and, in the case of legal width, provides those rules to the Market-Maker component described later on. Compliance Managers are only needed at the control sites.

Listener Components

We have four types of components whose main job is to collect market data from the outside and distribute it to other components; one each for stocks, options, futures, and news.

Stock Listener

This component connects with an exchange via a native API and listens to stock market data—current bids and offers as well as trade prints—published by the individual exchanges as well as the consolidated feed, filters out dubious ticks, then multicasts the scrubbed market data for other components. The dubious tick filtering is crucial. Of the hundreds of millions of ticks published each day, some of them are bound to be erroneous due to human or technical error or whatever. The last thing you want is for your system to use one of these bogus ticks to submit misinformed quotes or orders, which can be horribly costly. Note also that we publish not just the top of book but full-market depth. The Stock Listeners also publish the current state of each of their markets (ditto for Options and Futures Listeners).

Any securities market has a half-dozen or so states it can be in at any point in time. For example, at night most exchanges are *closed*, and during most of the day they are in an *open* state. Naturally you don't want your system attempting to trade when a market is not open. Another common state is the *fast* market state, typically for periods of unusually high volatility, during which the exchange may have modified rules for order allocations or whatnot. The stock listener is responsible for publishing the current state of its markets so other components can behave accordingly.

Options Listener
Just like the Stock Listener, but this component listens to each individual options exchange data feed, as well as the consolidated OPRA feed. Because there are orders of magnitude more option contracts than stocks, the Options Listener tends to get a lot busier than its stock counterpart.

Futures Listener
Same as the Stock and Options Listeners, listening to, scrubbing, and publishing equity index futures feeds, such as the all-important E-mini S&P 500 futures contract (ES). This component also publishes ticks for the also quite important Eurodollar (ED) futures traded at the CME. These futures allow one to borrow or lend money at the LIBOR rate for some future period of time at a specified interest rate. LIBOR is short for *London Interbank Offered Rate* and is widely used as a risk-free interest rate, which is one of the required inputs to pricing an option. As we'll see later, the Rate Curve Generator will use these Eurodollar futures prices to deduce these risk-free rates.

News Listener
This component listens to news feeds much the way a human trader might watch headlines on a Bloomberg screen, scanning for keywords indicating some event of interest—say, a company announcing a change in its dividend or an earnings announcement—likely to affect a stock price and/or option price. Once detected, the News Listener broadcasts the event to other components who might want to use that information. For example, a component implementing an event-driven trading strategy will certainly be a subscriber to such

news. The Option Pricer, discussed in the following section, is also likely to subscribe to any news regarding dividends, as changes in expected dividends affect the price of an option.

Pricer Components

The following components each contribute—directly or indirectly—to the calculation of theoretical prices for the securities we trade.

Implied Volatility Generator

The volatility of a stock price (or index) is a numerical representation of the frequency and magnitude of changes in the stock price (or index). It is also one of the most important factors in calculating the theoretical price of an option. The problem is that current volatility is, for all intents and purposes, impossible to measure directly.[8] You can, however, measure the volatility of a stock as *implied* by current option prices. And that's what this guy does, all day long. It continuously monitors the current market prices of options—bids, offers, and last trade prices—and uses an option pricing formula such as Black-Scholes in reverse, more or less.

That might sound weird, but hang on. The standard inputs to any option pricing formula are current stock price, expected dividends, strike price, time to expiration, risk-free interest rate, and volatility. Normally, you would collect all those inputs and run it through the formula to calculate an option price. But if you have option prices already and all inputs except for volatility, you can use a rearrangement of

---

[8] You can, of course, calculate historical volatility easily enough, but an option price requires the instantaneous volatility of a stock, or the volatility right now—not from a month or day or even one second ago.

the pricing formula to calculate the volatility required to produce that price (i.e., implied volatility).[9]

Volatility Curve Generator

As mentioned, one of the inputs to standard option pricing formulas is volatility. Now, it's impossible to overstate the importance of volatility to an options trader, especially an options market-maker. For all intents and purposes, volatility is the "price" of an option, and the premium expressed in dollars and cents is secondary. Options traders indeed often think not of buying or selling options but as buying or selling volatility. Whereas a profitable round-trip for a stock high-frequency trader might be buying 100 shares of some stock for $1.00 and selling them at $1.02, a good round-trip to an options high-frequency trader might be buying 100 options for 30 (volatility points) and selling them back at 32.

The job of the Volatility Curve Generator is to continuously calculate and publish volatilities for all strike prices and maturities of our stocks and indices, for use primarily by the Option Pricer. Volatilities are typically expressed in the form of curves. The most common curve is a simple x-y plot with the x, or horizontal axis, indicating strike price and the y, or vertical axis, indicating volatility. Figure 5.3 shows what it might look like.

A curve such as this indicates the volatility corresponding to any given strike price, and there are two essential inputs to producing a curve like this. One is implied volatility. The other is our current inventory, or positions, in option contracts corresponding to these strike prices. Think back to the basic lean your market strategy. The idea there is to facilitate

---

[9] The CBOE options calculator at cboe.com/LearnCenter/OptionCalculator .aspx has a nice feature that lets you calculate implied volatility—for educational use only—given a theoretical price and other input factors.

FIGURE 5.3

Volatility Curve

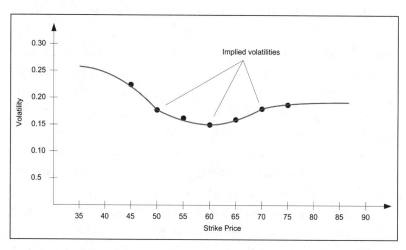

the completion of your round-trip, after a trade, by modifying your bid (after you sell) or offer (after you buy) in order to make you more attractive on that side of the market and therefore increase your likelihood of a round-tripping trade.

In options, this leaning can be done not only by modifying actual option prices, but by modifying the volatility curve. It's extraordinarily efficient to modify option prices this way because many option contracts require the same volatility (e.g., calls and puts on the same strike) in order to calculate their theoretical values, so you need only modify things in one place. And as just described, volatility *is* price. Should you buy a bunch of options (volatility) at some particular strike, to facilitate the round-trip you might very well lower the volatility at that area of the curve to make yourself more attractive as a seller (of volatility).

Once you get your head wrapped firmly around this concept of volatility as price, you may soon think of a potential third input to a volatility curve, something very much like alpha. Consider two volatility curves, one for options on the

S&P 500 index and another for the NASDAQ 100 index. Say you believe (as some high-frequency traders do) there is a lead-lag relationship between these two with respect to volatility (i.e., a volatility change in the former portends a change in the latter). Should implied volatility spike up in the S&P 500 curve for whatever reason, you may very quickly adjust your NASDAQ 100 curve upward in order to buy temporarily low-priced (in volatility terms) options, then sell them back when market prices (in volatility terms) adjust upward.

The curve in Figure 5.3 expresses volatilities for given strike prices. Another conventional type of curve expresses volatilities for different expiration dates. The Volatility Curve Generator may publish these two-dimensional strike and expiration curves separately, or it may combine them and publish volatilities in the form of a volatility surface, which we discussed in describing the volatility arbitrage strategy and looks something like Figure 5.4.

Rate Curve Generator

One of the inputs to any standard option pricing formula is a risk-free interest rate. This component continuously calculates and publishes these in the form of a rate curve, or yield curve, which, like the volatility curve, is a fairly simple x-y graph showing spot interest rates for any number of borrowing periods. Figure 5.5 is an example.

The Rate Curve Generator calculates spot interest rates based primarily on current market prices of Eurodollar futures, which trade at the Chicago Mercantile Exchange and are published by the Futures Listener.[10] There's a bit of tedious mathematics involved in the precise calculation, which goes something like this: A Eurodollar contract locks

---

[10] In addition to Eurodollars, we can also listen to U.S. Treasury security prices and imply interest rates from those.

FIGURE 5.4

Volatility Surface

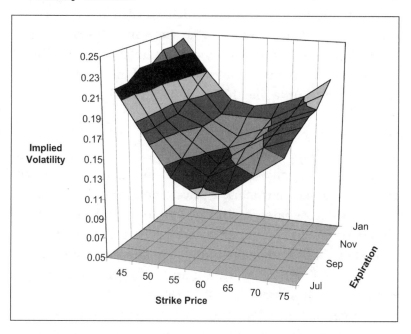

FIGURE 5.5

Interest Rate Curve

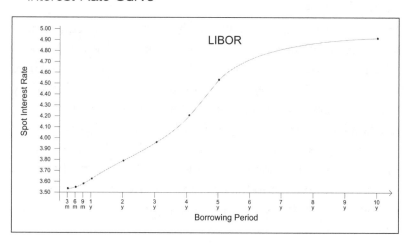

in a LIBOR rate for a borrowing period that begins some-time in the future. The prices of these contracts, then, imply forward interest rates, from which we can imply a corresponding spot rate, which is what we want. This component recalculates spot rates every time Eurodollars tick, then interpolates among the fixed maturity dates of these interest rates to construct a curve like the one in Figure 5.5.

Stock Pricer

This rather important component produces alpha-adjusted stock prices for all stocks we wish to trade. These prices are based on current market prices, published by the Stock Listener, and whatever strategy we are using to calculate alphas (these are described in the pairs trading strategy in an earlier chapter). For the futures lag strategy, for example, the Stock Pricer listens to the Futures Listener for changes in the S&P Futures price. Based on the direction and degree of change, and previously observed relationships between changes in stock price relative to changes in the index price (i.e., beta), it calculates an alpha factor, which it then uses to modify the current stock price.

Option Pricer

For each option contract we wish to trade, this component provides a current theoretical price for use by the Market-Maker. The theoretical price is based on current stock price (from the Stock Pricer), current volatility (from the Volatility Curve Generator), current risk-free interest rate (from the Rate Curve Generator), and expected dividends, strike price, and time-to-expiration (all from the Securities Manager). There are any number of option pricing formulas one might use to calculate option theoretical prices. The most well-known is, of course, the Black-Scholes formula, but it is limited for the most part to European options, or options that may only be exercised on the specified expiration date of the contract. For many American options, which may be exercised at any time up to and including expiration, one must use something like a binary tree formula. Another tree-based model is the trinomial tree, and a close cousin to that is the finite difference method, or FDM. It's beyond the scope of this book to get into the details here (there are gobs of books out there that do quite a fantastic job of that), but for our hypothetical system, we'll go with FDM. It's an extraordinarily efficient model and lends itself nicely to parallel processing, which we like to take advantage of wherever we can.

Regardless of what formula you use, the recalculation of an option price—say, after the stock price ticks—takes time. To reduce this time, we'll borrow a technique that goes back to the early days of floor-based options trading. The two pricing factors likely to change most frequently are the underlier price and underlier volatility. What we'll do, then, say, at the start of each day, is precalculate option theoretical prices for a range of underlier prices and volatilities, centering that range of current levels. We will repeat that for all strike prices (and expirations) we wish to trade. Then as the underlier price, say, actually moves, the Option Pricer need not recalculate the theoretical price but simply look it up from its three-dimensional grid or cube of precalculated theoretical prices.

This is precisely analogous to what floor traders used to do. Each morning, they or their clerks would print out thick sets of "sheets," as they were known, with theoretical prices for ranges of underlier prices and volatilities. The traders would look at these sheets throughout the day (getting new ones as needed, as when underlier prices moved off the range of precalculated theoretical prices) and know at a glance current theoretical prices without having to do a recalcula-

FIGURE 5.6

Option Price Cube

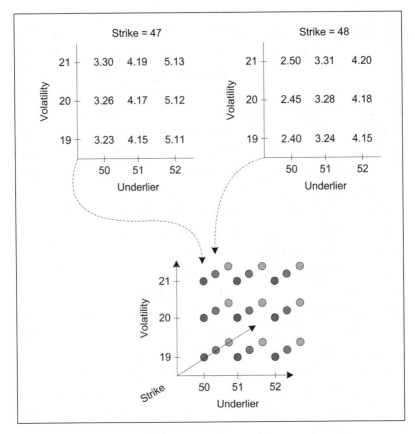

tion. Calculating these cubes is not quite as easy as it might seem. For one, even precalculation takes time, so you can't practically precalculate for every possible underlier price and volatility level. Instead you choose some reasonable, discrete set of these, calculate for them, then interpolate among them to return a theoretical price for any conceivable underlier price or volatility. Then the challenge is to not interpolate *too* much, for that reduces the accuracy of the interpolated prices. But if you overdo it the other way, you spend so much time precalculating that you lose the benefit you're after in the first place. Figure 5.6 illustrates the concept of a precalculated price cube.[11]

Market-Maker

This component calculates a generic bid-ask spread for each stock and option, based on current market, instructions from the Strategy Server, and prices from the Stock Pricer and Option Pricer. For stocks, it will also consider current positions (inventory) and lean markets accordingly. For options markets, the inventory adjustment is already built in to the option price by way of the volatility curve as described earlier. Option bid-ask prices will also take into consideration such factors as the cost of hedging the option trade, the cost of financing the option trade (e.g., cost of borrowing money to pay premium for a purchase), and the "volatility of volatility." (Recalling again that volatility is a proxy for price, the market-maker requires more compensation for taking positions in options with frequently changing volatility than for options with more stable volatilities.)

Trader Components

The components that interact directly with the external world for trade execution consist of quoting engines, electronic eyes (including a special one just for option spreads), a stock locator, and a hedger.

Stock Quoting Engine

The Stock Quoting Engine is responsible for transmitting markets (bid and offer prices with corresponding sizes) from

---

[11] These prices were generated by the CBOE options calculator at cboe .com/LearnCenter/OptionCalculator.aspx for American-style call options on a non–dividend paying stock with 30 days until expiration and an annual interest rate of 2 percent.

the Market-Maker to an individual exchange. As with the Listeners, this component is custom-written for the API of a given exchange, and as such, we will have an entirely unique quoting engine per exchange (i.e., no FIX). While in concept the transmission of quotes into an exchange-matching engine seems simple enough, in practice it is one very tedious task indeed. Each exchange has its own nuances with respect to how many quotes it will accept in a given package of quotes, how frequently it will accept new quotes, and how it signals receipt of quotes back to the quoting engine. It's extraordinarily important to get these nuances right because quotations are binding obligations to trade, and quotes must be updated almost continuously. Should you want to change a quote but fail to do so for whatever reason, you are very likely to see someone else trade against your quote, forcing you to eat a bad trade.

Another responsibility of our Stock Quoting Engine is the proper setting of safety controls that most exchanges have in place to protect the Market-Maker from some (but not all) unintentional trading. For example, the exchange may let you specify that after X number of fills in Y seconds, the exchange will automatically nullify any quotes you have in the markets, preventing further fills. Another common example is known as heartbeat monitoring. The idea here is that the quoting engine sends a simple message—a heartbeat—to the exchange on some interval simply indicating that the quoting engine is functional, or alive. Should the exchange stop detecting the heartbeat, it will assume trouble on your side and remove your quotes from the market.

Stock Electronic Eye

The Stock Electronic Eye, or EE, is similar to the Stock Quoting Engine in that it transmits orders to a specific exchange—again using native APIs—according to bid/ask prices and sizes from the Market-Maker and instructions from the Strategy Server. (For example, the Strategy Server will likely tell the EE whether or not to use tighter markets than the quoting engine does.) Whereas a quoting engine will transmit limit orders (which are essentially the same as quotes), the EE shoots only IOC, or immediate-or-cancel, orders. Unlike the passive trading done by the quoting engine, the EE is all about active trading.

Option Quoting Engine
Identical to the Stock Quoting Engine, but for options.

Option Electronic Eye
Identical to the Stock Electronic Eye, but for options exchanges.

Option Spreader
This component is like the Option EE in that it fires IOC orders on the options book, but the book here is not of individual options but of standard combinations of options known as *spreads* or *strategies*. Whereas an individual option is used for some relatively simple purpose, such as insuring against a steep decline in the value of some stock you hold, spreads can be used for things like insuring against a stock price moving out of some range of prices or moving significantly above or below some particular price—in other words, of undergoing high volatility. An example of the latter is known as a *straddle* (as discussed in Chapter 3), which consists of one call option and one put option, each with the same strike price. This spread can be used to reduce a portfolio's exposure to volatility, a measure known as vega. The Option Spreader monitors spread books, such as the complex order book, or COB, at the Chicago Board Options Exchange, and attempts to trade them as directed by the Strategy Server.

Stock Locator

To sell a stock short, one borrows someone else's shares then sells them with the intention of buying them back at some point before returning them. There are many different reasons for short selling. The high-frequency stock trader, for example, will sell short when he wishes to hit a bid but doesn't have the stock to sell. And the high-frequency options trader will sell short in order to delta-hedge certain option trades. Regardless of why you are shorting, it is generally required (or at least a very good idea) that you indeed borrow shares before selling them short.[12] The job of the Stock Locator component is to do just that. It uses connections to brokerage firms (the typical source of shares for borrowing) to ensure there is a ready supply of borrowed shares. We only need one of these at the control sites.

Auto Hedger

Recall from the description of the jump the delta strategy how an options market-maker will typically follow the trading of an option with the trading of some number of shares of the underlying stock in order to delta-hedge the option position. This is the component that does that. The basic idea is to trade some number of shares (buying or selling short) following an option trade, according to the delta of the option calculated at the time of the trade. In practice, there are other considerations. First and foremost, the delta of an option changes over time in the same way that its theoretical price changes. As such, a hedge position must be rebalanced from time to time according to changes in delta. So the Auto Hedger must continuously monitor the delta of the option position and trade stock as needed to maintain delta neutrality. Also,

---

[12] To short without borrowing is known as naked short selling and is more than a little bit controversial.

when an option expires or is exercised or assigned,[13] or if an option trade is busted or adjusted (see Position Manager in the "Manager Components" section), any corresponding stock position must generally be modified as well.

Now, as we know only too well, the options market-maker attempting to delta-hedge in this conventional manner is subject to the sharp eyes of the high-frequency trader attempting to trade stock in front of the options market-maker. For this reason, some options market-makers will hedge not with the underlying stock but with an index security such as the Spider ETF (if the stock is among the S&P 500 names). Doing so is a bit trickier, as the number of ETF shares required is based not only on the delta of the option but also on the beta[14] of the underlying stock, but if the market-maker wants to keep from getting nibbled by the delta jumpers, he or she may have no choice.

Other than delta-hedging, which attempts to counterbalance the effect of an option value's sensitivity to changes in the underlier, the Auto Hedger is also responsible for *rho-hedging*. Rho measuress the sensitivity of an option value to changes in the risk-free interest rate; as interest rates change, so do option values. One can hedge this exposure in a manner very similar to delta-hedging; however, the hedging instrument in this case is the Eurodollar futures contract (review Rate Curve Generator) and the guiding measure is

---

[13] The concept of assignment pertains only to holders of short option positions, i.e., option writers. When a holder of a long option decides to exercise, the exchange will choose some option writer to honor their obligation to sell or buy the underlier (in the case of calls or puts, respectively) to or from the exerciser. The chosen writer is in this manner said to be assigned.

[14] Recall that *beta* is a measure of how a stock price changes relative to changes in the market overall, or, more practically speaking, relative to an index of which the stock is a component.

rho, which, like delta, changes over time and must be reconsidered and potentially rehedged.

Manager Components

The following manager components sit off to the side, if you will, taking care of important monitoring and reporting functions.

Fuse Box

Our HFT system, at any moment in time during trading hours, will have upward of a million quotes in the U.S. markets, each of them an obligation to trade at those prices. The system will, of course, modify those quotes more or less continuously throughout the day in order to ensure that we really do want to trade at those prices. This exposes us to an enormous risk. Should we fail to update those quotes as quickly as possible, others will be only too happy to trade with us at those bad prices, or "pick us off," as it's known. Now, with a system as complex as this one, there are any number of possible sources of problems that might lead us to having bad quotes in the market. And, with the speeds at which market prices change, there is no time for a human to monitor for such problems before getting picked off. As such, we need a system component whose sole responsibility is to monitor for any potential condition we can think of and, upon detection of such a condition, automatically inform other components to modify their behavior accordingly.

An example of such a condition is the loss of a market data feed. Without knowing current market prices, it is virtually impossible to know what prices you should trade at. When the Fuse Box detects the loss of a market data feed, it will send messages to all trading components and instruct them to cease trading. The autoquoter, for example, may react to this condition by either pulling its quotes from the market or temporarily widening them to all but guarantee they won't be filled. Other conditions might include the reaching of a position limit, an unusually rapid fill rate (trading more than X contracts or shares, say, in Y seconds time), the occurrence of a bad trade, or the failure of a crucial system component such as a Listener or Pricer.

Trade Log

The job of this component is as simple as its name implies. It maintains a detailed log of every trade the system makes. For each trade, it maintains the security traded, price traded, whether bought or sold, which exchange it traded on, and (if the exchange provides it) the identity of the counterparty.

Position Manager

Like the Trade Log, the job of this component is also rather simple but crucially important. The Position Manager simply listens for trades, maintains a running position for each security traded by the system, and publishes those positions as they change. And note it's more than just trading that can modify a position. It's not unusual for an exchange, at the end of a day, to inform someone his trade is being busted (erased, as if it never happened) or adjusted (size or price modified). Trade busts and adjustments are typically the result of a so-called obvious error either by the exchange itself or one of the counterparties.[15] For option positions, the Position Manager must also take expiration, exercise, and assignments into account, each of which results in a change to the position.

---

[15] Most exchanges have "obvious error" provisions that allow a party who did a bad trade to petition the exchange for a trade bust or adjustment. These petitions typically must be received within a certain number of minutes of the trade, and for professional traders are not always honored as they often require the consent of the counterparty.

Risk Manager

Consider the essential quest of the high-frequency trader: to buy at one price then sell at a higher one. The Risk Manager is all about what happens during the "then" period, or the financial risk of the high-frequency trader while waiting to complete his round-trips. It measures, from moment to moment, the financial risk of our positions. Imagine the high-frequency trader who wishes to buy stock PDQ for $1.00 and sell it for $1.01. Now consider the sequence presented in Table 5.2.

After the first trade, the trader has put up $500 to buy the stock. That $500, like any stock investment, is at risk. Should the stock decline in price, the trader will lose money, potentially all of it. His cash at risk, or exposure, is $500. After the second trade, his position is down to 100 shares and so is his cash at risk (the profit he made on the trade is irrelevant for our purposes here). After the third trade, the exposure grows to $200, then to $600 after the fourth trade. The chief purpose of the Risk Manager is to keep track of these exposures for every stock we trade. But our Risk Manager does more than simply monitor these exposures. When an exposure exceeds a preset threshold, it makes trades automatically to reduce it. Imagine our threshold exposure for PDQ is $800 and the sequence continues as in Table 5.3.

After the trade at time 6, the Risk Manager recognizes that our PDQ position is beyond the threshold level of $800.

TABLE 5.2

Trading Risk Scenario 1

Time 1	Buy 500 shares PDQ for $1.00	$500 at risk
Time 2	Sell 400 shares PDQ for $1.02	$100 at risk
Time 3	Buy 100 shares PDQ for $1.00	$200 at risk
Time 4	Buy 400 shares PDQ for $1.00	$600 at risk

TABLE 5.3

Trading Risk Scenario 2

Time 5	Buy 100 shares PDQ for $1.00	$700 at risk
Time 6	Buy 200 shares PDQ for $1.00	$900 at risk
Time 7	Sell 100 shares PDQ for $0.99	$800 at risk

At time 7, it automatically sells 100 shares—at a loss—in order to bring the exposure back to its limit. In this scenario, we still have a net gain at this point of $0.01 ($0.02 gain from trade 2, less $0.01 loss from trade 7), but we can think of that here as good luck. The Risk Manager is chiefly concerned with managing the exposure. Had it been required to sell at a loss of $0.02 or even more, it still would have done the risk-reducing trade.

For options, the job of the Risk Manager is rather more complex. A stock portfolio has only one source of risk: the market price of the stock. An options portfolio, however, is sensitive not only to the market price of the stock (delta, in options parlance) but to other factors as well. The basic exposures are given by the remaining Greeks: gamma (second-order delta), vega (sensitivity to changes in volatility), theta (sensitivity to change in time), and rho (sensitivity to changes in the risk-free interest rate). As we know, the Auto Hedger takes care of both delta- and rho-hedging, but the Risk Manager will nonetheless calculate each of these exposures more or less continuously, at least display them to human traders and risk managers, and make them available to other components (e.g., the Fuse Box).

In addition to calculating risk exposures based on current market conditions, the Risk Manager also performs nonstop "what if" analysis, calculating risk measures under various scenarios. For example, it is likely to calculate the delta measure (for both stocks and options) for a range of potential underlier prices, both above and below the current price. In this way, human traders can see what their risk will grow to based on how the market moves. This component is clearly one of the more indispensible of our system. As such, we deploy it at not only the control site but at each remote site as well.

P&L Calculator

We'll no doubt wonder, as our whirligig contraption does its thing, whether or not we are making any money. The job of the P&L Calculator is to answer that question. The basic daily P&L (profit and loss) calculation for any trading operation goes like this: For every security you trade, take the difference between the end-of-day value and beginning-of-day value. For securities traded that day, use the trade price instead of beginning-of-day price (since you didn't have it at the beginning of the day) and subtract any costs (exchange fees, etc.). If you want to do this intraday, use the current value instead of end-of-day value. That's the daily P&L for that security. Net those all together, and there's the overall daily P&L for your operation. That's basically it, and we need not do this at remote sites, only the control sites.

In most shops, there are two types of P&L calculation, sometimes known as front-office P&L versus back-office P&L. The former uses theoretical values as calculated by the system for trading purposes, while the latter uses "mark to market" values based on prices actually observed in the market. Over the long run, these two generally match up, but from one day to the next, it's not uncommon to see a difference.

There are zillion different ways one can report P&L. You might calculate it per trading desk, or per time period, or asset class, or whatever. But the basic calculation is the same. For options P&L, it's also helpful to attribute P&L per Greek. For example, your "delta P&L" is a good measure of how effectively you are delta-hedging, "vega P&L" a measure of your volatility management, and so on. Knowing these attributions can be very helpful in tuning your system.

INTERACTION SCENARIO

Now that we know what all the components are and what each of them does, let's see how they interact and get work done. Doing so for every possible interaction would fill many books, so we'll just look at what happens when the ES futures gap, or change by a substantial amount. It turns out this will exercise a fair number of system components and also demonstrate both the futures lag strategy in the stock market and the take out slow movers strategy in options, both explained in Chapter 3. (In practice, it could also kick off the futures versus ETF strategy.) For simplicity, we'll assume the stock scenario plays out only at one remote site for only a small number of stocks and option contracts. In practice, the scenarios would play out independently at every exchange site, with trades on many more stocks and options.

Time 1, 2, 3

The very first thing to happen is a sudden change in the ES futures price, say from $1,162.00 to $1,162.50. Figure 5.7 illustrates the initial component interactions in response to the change.

It's the job of the Futures Listener to detect the gap and publish the new price, but the job is not quite as easy as it might seem. The Listener has to do more than simply publish

FIGURE 5.7

Futures Gap Scenario—Times 1 to 3

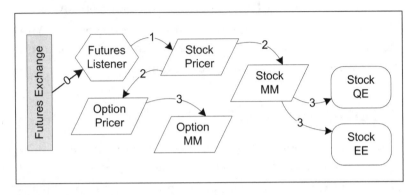

every new tick that comes in from the exchange. Instead, it must apply some intelligence to be certain that new prices are, first, reasonable, and not likely to be erroneous. In addition to filtering out bad ticks, it must also exercise judgment in not necessarily publishing every good tick as it comes in. If prices fluctuate rapidly between two price levels, or flutter, there is no point publishing each of those ticks lest the downstream components also get caught up in excessive recalculation and whatnot. Consider the hypothetical stream of last-sale ES prices (i.e., these are neither bids nor offers, but prices at which trades actually occurred) in Table 5.4.[16]

Assume the last price published by the Futures Listener before this stream was 1162.00, so that's the current price of the ES as far as the rest of the system is concerned when the Listener starts evaluating this stream. First off, the 1152.00 price at time 2:30:21 is so far from the previous tick that our listener will deem it bad and ignore it. How about the 1162.25

---

[16] This is quite a simplified view, for illustration. An actual time-of-sale stream might include far more ticks than these, changing at much smaller intervals than the whole-second increments we use here.

TABLE 5.4

E-Mini S&P 500 Futures Price Stream

Time	Price	Qty
02:30:21 P.M.	1162.00	1
02:30:21 P.M.	1152.00	5
02:30:22 P.M.	1162.00	10
02:30:24 P.M.	1162.25	350
02:30:24 P.M.	1162.00	50
02:30:26 P.M.	1162.00	10
02:30:28 P.M..	1162.25	50
02:30:28 P.M.	1162.25	100
02:30:28 P.M.	1162.50	71
02:30:28 P.M.	1162.75	200
02:30:29 P.M.	1162.75	50
02:30:29 P.M.	1162.75	150
02:30:30 P.M.	1162.75	5
02:30:30 P.M.	1162.75	12

at 2:30:24, for a relatively large size of 350? Neither will our listener publish this because the very next price is back to 1162.00, as is the next tick. It ignores that as well. But look what happens starting at 2:30:28. The price goes up a quarter as before, goes up another quarter on the next tick, and goes up even another quarter in the very next tick to 1162.75. And it stays there. Our Listener deems this valid and publishes a new ES price of 1162.75, a full 75 cents greater than the last published price. (Note we are using intentionally simplistic logic here for illustration. Actual logic for tick analysis and publishing can get a lot more sophisticated than this.)

Looking again at Figure 5.7, we see the Stock Pricer receives the new price at time 1. The job of the Pricer, for the purposes of this scenario, is to deduce a corresponding microprice for each of the stocks in the S&P 500 index based on the relative weight of the component and its beta, which, if you recall, is roughly indicative of the correlation between changes in a stock price relative to changes in the overall market, represented in this case by the index. At time 2, the Stock Pricer publishes each of these new microprices.

Next, the Stock Market-Maker uses the new microprices to calculate new bid and offer prices for each component stock, and the Option Pricer uses them to look up new option theoretical prices from its price cube. At time 3, the Stock Market-Maker publishes new stock markets and the Option Pricer publishes new theoretical prices. Notice the natural lag between stock and option pricing, since the latter is a derivative of the former.

Time 4, 5

As illustrated in Figure 5.8, at time 4, the Stock Electronic Eye takes out any market bids and/or offers of slow movers that interact with our new markets (i.e., takes out prices with alpha). The Stock Quoting Engine simultaneously updates

FIGURE 5.8

Futures Gap Scenario—Times 4, 5

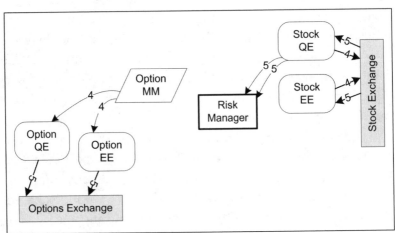

our own bids and offers, making us relatively attractive buyers or sellers on the other side of the market taken out by the EE to facilitate completion of round-trips. Also at time 4, the Option Market-Maker publishes new bid and offer prices.

At time 5, the stock trading engines receive fills back from the exchange. The Risk Manager verifies that each buy of a stock is matched with a sale at a higher price, for a corresponding number of shares. (Were this not the case, and if the position exceeded preset limits, the Risk Manager would send messages back to the Stock EE to make trades to reduce exposures.) Also at time 5, the Option Quoting Engine updates its bids and offers on the options exchange and the Option EE sends take-out orders on slow-mover market bids and offers that interact with our new markets.

Time 6

As illustrated in Figure 5.9, at time 6, the options trading engines relay trade fills to both the Risk Manager and the Auto Hedger. Unlike the stock trades, the option trades do not round-trip with each other (i.e., we don't have matching buys and sells of the same contracts as we did with stock).

FIGURE 5.9

Futures Gap Scenario—Time 6

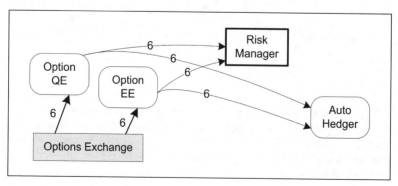

Time 7, 8, 9

As illustrated in Figure 5.10, at time 7, the Auto Hedger calculates the delta exposure from the option trades and sends the appropriate trade orders to the stock exchange to neutralize the delta. At the same time, the Risk Manager determines that our vega exposures have exceeded preset limits with this latest batch of option trades. It publishes a message indicating the excessive exposure. At time 8, the Option Spreader picks up that message and places an order on the spread order book at the option exchange for an option straddle. At time 9, the exchange sends a successful fill notification back to the Option Spreader, which forwards it back to the Risk Manager, which determines that vega is again within acceptable limits.[17]

FIGURE 5.10

Futures Gap Scenario—Times 7 to 9

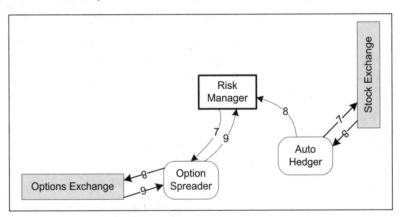

---

[17] Note there are many other ways to hedge volatility exposure beyond the simple straddle, beginning with other common option spreads such as butterflies and calendar spreads. For hedging market-wide vega, one can also take advantage of volatility swaps in the OTC market or the VX futures contract traded at the CBOE.

FIGURE 5.11

Futures Gap Scenario

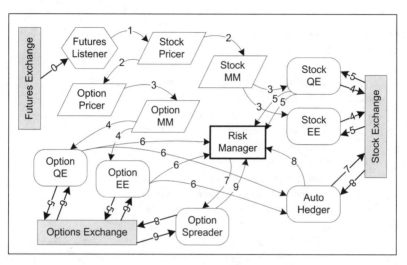

Putting It All Together

Figure 5.11 shows the complete scenario from start to finish and Table 5.5, which follows, lays out a summary of what happens during each time interval. Notice we left the actions of the Trade Log and Position Manager, listed in Table 5.5, out of the illustrations to keep them from getting entirely too crazy. And remember the entire process is replicated at each of our remote sites, in order to take advantage of opportunities on every stock and options exchange, so all Risk Managers must take into consideration trade fills from all remote sites, another important interaction required in practice.

DASHBOARD

There's another element of the HFT system we've not described, but its importance cannot be overstated. Think of it like a dashboard on a car. This is the set of screens and whatnot for the humans who must monitor the system as it

TABLE 5.5

Component Interactions in Response to Futures Gap

Time 1	Futures Listener detects ES gap, publishes new price
Time 2	Stock Pricer calculates and publishes new theoretical prices
Time 3	Stock Market-Maker recalculates markets
	Option Pricer looks up and publishes new theoretical prices
Time 4	Stock EE fires on market offers
	Stock Quoting Engine moves stock bids and offers
	Option Market-Maker recalculates markets
	Option Pricer starts rebalancing matrices
Time 5	Stock EE receives/publishes stock EE fills
	Stock Quoting Engine receives/publishes quote fills
	Option EE takes out market bids and offers
	Option Quoting Engine moves option bids and offers
Time 6	Trade Log records Stock EE and quoter fills
	Position Manager updates stock positions
	Option EE receives/publishes EE fills
	Option Quoting Engine receives/publishes quote fills
Time 7	Trade Log records Option EE and quoter fills
	Auto Hedger calculates deltas and sends stock trade orders
	Risk Manager calculates position vega, publishes limit violation
Time 8	Auto Hedger receives/publishes stock fills
	Option Spreader sends straddle trade order
Time 9	Trade Log records auto hedger stock fills
	Option Spreader receives/publishes straddle fill
Time 10	Trade Log records straddle fill

does its thing, just as any driver of a car requires human controls and displays laid out just so on a dashboard. The graphical user interfaces, or GUIs ("gooeys"), allow traders to do things like enter parameters for the Strategy Server to relay to the appropriate components, see trades and positions as they occur, see position risks in real time—to verify that the Risk Managers are doing their job—shut off the system in an emergency (every trader screen has a ready "Panic" button to accommodate this crucial requirement), enter trade adjustments manually when the exchange reports a trade bust or modification, and much more. And the trade support team requires windows into the inner workings of the components. For example, a system like this never—ever—runs perfectly smoothly. As the system does its thing, components report a steady stream of anomalies and/or errors, some requiring remediation and some not, and the dashboard must have a means of alerting the right people of these.

CLOSING THE HOOD

So there's our look under the hood of an HFT system. It's only a sketch, of course, and we've clearly made simplifying assumptions for the sake of clarity. Mostly we've exposed some gaping "latency holes" that a real HFT system will attempt to fill. For example, we assume that an Option Pricer cannot start repricing until a new microprice is available, and the crafty HFT system designer will no doubt think of ways to reduce the delay to virtually nothing. We also assume our components are organized functionally, with different components responsible for different functions but able to perform those functions for any security. Another possible architecture builds components around very small sets of securities—say ten stocks—but has individual components do everything from listening to market data to repricing to shooting trade orders and managing risk. Our sample inter-action scenario also has a few simplifying assumptions (e.g., the perfectly matched stock trades and the availability of a suitable number of option straddles to perfectly reduce vega), but it does give an idea of the nontrivial amount of interaction required to pull off a comparatively simple HFT strategy.

We also assume our system gets all this work done very, very quickly. The futures lag interaction, for example, can be completed in a matter of 100 milliseconds, and a good deal of that time is spent waiting for the exchanges to return fills. And by the time you read this book, high-frequency traders may be getting it all done even much faster than that. Nobody can say how many high-frequency traders attempt the futures lag strategy, but it's safe to say it's being done. And only one of those firms can be the fastest. If you're not the fastest, it's hardly worth the bother of attempting it. Fortunately, there are always methods of optimizing a system just a teensy bit more and a steady supply of new technology to do the same.

CHAPTER 6

The High-Frequency Trading Debate

Does high-frequency trading make the markets better? Its defenders think so, and there are reasonable arguments one can make in supporting their case. But there are plenty of equally reasonable concerns about HFT as well. We'll attempt to summarize the debate with an important caveat emptor: there's not a lot of evidence to go on—at least not yet. With hope, we can look forward to more research and study and other insights into this only recently discovered corner of the financial markets. But the following is some of what we have so far.

BENEFITS

Defenders of HFT list tighter, deeper markets; price consistency; and the lack of panic on the part of computers as benefits. We'll examine each of these claims.

Tighter, Deeper Markets

It's presumably beyond debate that the technological capabilities of high-frequency traders have advanced considerably in recent years and that there are more and more firms getting into the game. It's not unreasonable to see how this would lead to the purported HFT benefit most often repeated, that HFT facilitates liquidity by facilitating tighter markets (smaller bid-ask spreads) and deeper markets (bigger sizes). As we already know, with all else equal, tighter markets are better for investors than wider markets because buying investors pay less and selling investors receive more. And with greater sizes, there are more securities available at those superior prices.

Imagine an ultrasimplified market in which there are but two market-makers and each has just bought 1,000 shares of stock for one dollar. Each wants to complete his round-trip, selling 1,000 shares to eliminate the risk of holding his position open. Market-maker A offers $1.10 in hopes of earning a dime spread. Market-maker B offers $1.09, content with the prospect of a penny less, to make himself more attractive to buyers. Market-maker A sees that and decides eight cents would be better than nothing and improves accordingly to $1.08. Market-maker B improves to $1.07. A improves to $1.06. And so on.

In the days before decimalization, the limit to this improvement was one-eighth of a dollar, or just over 12 cents. But with pricing increments for most stocks reduced to a penny, or even one-hundredth of a penny for stocks trading at less than a dollar, the competition among market-makers can rapidly collapse spreads to almost nothing. Now imagine adding many more market-makers, each bent on completing his or her round-trip, and you can appreciate how markets not only tighten but become deeper as well.

Price Consistency

If you want to buy stock in Google, Coca-Cola, General Electric, or probably any other company you can think of off the top of your head, you (or your broker) needn't think much about which of the dozen or so exchanges and ATSs to go to as far as price is concerned. There's no point shopping around because you can be very sure the price will be virtually the same, instant by instant, anywhere the stock trades. This is, of course, due to our good friend the arbitrageur, who keeps a very close lookout for price differences across markets and trades them out of existence—buying the lower-priced while selling the higher-priced—in a matter of microseconds.[1]

Owing to the eternal attraction of free money, you can bet there is no shortage of well-armed HFT firms making sure no simple arbitrage like this goes unnoticed. And it's not just the simple arbitrageur at work here, making sure the same stock trades at the same price everywhere. The pairs-trading predictor keeps prices of highly correlated stocks in sync with each other as well. Were it suddenly discovered, for instance, that high-fructose corn syrup can cause Sudden Incontinence Syndrome or some other such malady, you can be certain that the stocks of all affected companies[2] would move accordingly and quite simultaneously due to the lightning-speed actions of the HFT crowd.

Computers Don't Panic

It's interesting to speculate, whenever there is a massive stock sell-off or downright crash, how much of the dip is due to people just freaking out. It's human nature to run for the doors when everyone else seems to be, and equally natural

---

[1] To give full credit where it is due, the SEC can also take some credit for keeping stock prices consistent across markets as a result of well-known Regulation NMS and its NBBO trade-through protections.

[2] And they are legion, as anyone who has read Michael Pollan's *The Omnivore's Dilemma* well knows.

for some people's fear to make them sell their stock when it tanks, for no rational reason. Say what you will about them, but automated trading systems don't succumb to emotion like that. Granted, they make mistakes—we'll get to that point presently when we discuss rogue trading—but for the most part, they only trade when they recognize clear and convincing signs they should do so.

Indeed, a strong case can be made that not only do automated trading systems avoid making this uniquely human mistake, but they can mitigate the negative consequences when the humans do succumb to panic. Plenty of HFT systems consider the so-called fundamentals of a company—sales, earnings, dividends, and the like—when determining a reasonable range for a company's stock price. Should a wild and likely bogus rumor pound down the price of a stock, the fundamental trader is likely to buy up all he can, knowing with some degree of confidence the price will rebound. Similarly, should a price rally like mad due to clearly erroneous news, the fundamental trader will sell it short and wait for sensibility to bring the price down again, when he'll close out his short position for a nice profit.

CONCERNS

HFT detractors name price manipulation, colocation, volatility, rogue trading, and other risks and concerns. As we did with benefits, let's examine each objection in turn.

Price Manipulation

When the high-frequency trader tows an iceberg or pushes an elephant, he is quite unabashedly attempting to move prices for his own benefit and against the best interest of the party behind the order. And while the practices may be legal (and presumably are legal, but don't take my word for it), you won't have to look far for someone who thinks the practice reeks of slime. It seems so unethical. Like cheating. Like taking advantage of someone who just wants to trade at the current market price and doesn't deserve to be yanked around like that. The high-frequency trader has a ready response to criticism like this, one we might call the stupidity defense: if someone is stupid enough to put out an order likely to move the market or to use an easily detected strategy like the iceberg, then that person deserves to be taken advantage of. The defense may not get the guy past the pearly gates of heaven, but you have to acknowledge its rationality.

As we've seen, it's not just the market-maker who is unafraid to move a market for his own best interest. Earlier, we noted how the investor can fool the penny jumper by making it seem like she wants to trade on one side of the market when her real interest is on the other side. That investor submits shill orders with no real desire that they be filled only to keep the market from moving away from her. Could that be deemed manipulative trading? Some assert that it could.

Increased Volatility

The volatility of a market is a measure of, to use a technical term, changiness. Although it can be measured quantitatively, we needn't bother and can just think of volatility as how frequently and how dramatically prices change. Although *volatility* refers literally to price changes in either direction, when people speak of volatility in the markets they tend to refer to price decreases. If one year a market increases by 10 percent and the next year it decreases by 10 percent, the latter year is considered more volatile. Go figure. We point out this semantic only to clarify what critics likely are referring to when they posit that HFT unnecessarily and excessively increases market volatility. Is it true?

I'm unaware of any compelling empirical evidence supporting the claim that HFT is responsible for increased volatility, but intuitively it has more than a ring of plausibility. high-frequency trading algorithms do their thing by necessity at great speed. And at great scale, too, because any individual trade is likely to make the high-frequency trader only a fraction of a penny. He needs lots and lots of trading to make back his investment in all the cool computing gear and well-paid programmers and quantitative analysts. Add to this the sheer and growing number of firms independently engaged in HFT, each with their own particular strategies and inventories and agendas, all running at full throttle and taking big gulps all the time. Those agendas are bound to interact with one another and, occasionally, it would seem, in ways that move a market price much more rapidly and farther than it otherwise would. Imagine two racetracks, one with three cars furiously circling the infield and the other with three hundred. Where are you more likely to see a collision?

The other thing to keep in mind with respect to volatility is how much high-frequency traders love it. When prices are on the move, one way or the other, it's easier to make those round-trips than when markets are slow. If you believe markets are falling, you're more willing to sell short because you're confident you can buy it back at a lower price. Same when markets are rallying, when you're more willing to buy believing you can sell back at a higher price. More trades, more spreads, more rebates.

And it's not just stock market-makers. Options market-makers absolutely love high volatility. Volatility (quantified into a number) is arguably the most important input to an option-pricing formula. Volatility can also be seen as a measure of uncertainty. And simplifying things here, but really not by much, the more volatility (actually the volatility of volatility itself, if you can get your head around that), the more uncertainty there is about the true theoretical price of an option and thus the wider the spreads. And we already know that wide markets are better for market-makers than for investors. The volatility storm in the waning months of 2008 was crazy for most everyone else, but it was a once-in-a-career windfall for quite a few high-frequency options traders.

Beyond this theoretical conjecturing, there's also more than a bit of empirical evidence suggesting that high-frequency trading accelerates volatility to the real loss of money for the individual investor. Consider the case below, as reported by Matt Goldstein of Reuters, of an investor losing several thousand dollars despite having what seemed like an appropriate safeguard in place:

> *On April 28, Watson was caught in a freak trading storm as shares of Dendreon plummeted 69 percent in 70 seconds. The Seattle biotech's stock plunged to $7.50 from $24, as the company got ready to provide investors with an update on its experimental prostate cancer treatment drug.*
>
> *In little over a minute, the equivalent of an entire day's worth of trading activity in Dendreon's shares took place before the NASDAQ stock market halted the stock.*
>
> *By then the damage was done. The lightning-fast selling triggered a so-called stop-loss standing order Watson had with his broker to sell Dendreon shares if the stock fell into the low $20s. But the stock fell so fast that the broker didn't actually sell Watson's 1,500 shares until the price had hit $15.*[3]

---

[3] Matt Goldstein, "The Victims of High-Frequency Trading," Reuters Breaking views, October 12, 2009, blogs.reuters.com/columns/2009/10/12/the-victims-of-HF-trading.

It's no smoking gun, but it requires no stretch of the imagination to figure at least some of Dendreon's plunge was due to high-frequency trading, given how quickly it happened. If HFT was indeed responsible for even some of the outrageous volatility of 2008, then considering the staggering cumulative losses that year, it would be downright painful to estimate how much of the hit taken by countless college funds and retirement accounts was due to the millionaire birthing operation of high-frequency trading.

Trading for Trading's Sake

It's said that up to 70 percent of all trading volume can now be attributed to high-frequency trading. If that's even remotely true, and if a sizeable amount of that is just HFT firms trading with other HFT firms, then it makes one wonder, what the heck is the point? You can imagine how this strikes many observers as a sign of something wrong with this picture. For example, is all of this trading between noninvestors just overtaxing the system?

One of the ongoing dilemmas in automated trading circles is the ever-increasing network bandwidth required to keep up with the explosion in market data over the past several years. If that additional traffic is attributable to HFT–HFT trades, then why should non-HFT firms have to incur the costs of more bandwidth? And are the exchanges incurring additional overhead costs to service all this trading activity, costs passed ultimately back to investors? It makes one wonder about the real purpose of a securities exchange. Is the presumed mission of providing fairly priced liquidity to the investing public being eclipsed by wealth-generation for the middlemen?

A related concern here is the notion that high-frequency traders don't hold onto their stock, that once they buy it they want to sell it as quickly as possible, or vice versa, and will flip the same stock positions hundreds or thousands of times in a single day. Although this is an oft-raised concern, one that makes some people scratch their heads, once you know what market-making is all about, then it makes sense. Wal-Mart doesn't want to hold onto its inventory any longer than it has to, nor does any retailer. And for the same reason, the market-maker doesn't want to hold his position any longer than he has to.

The classic market-maker wants to provide the service of facilitating a trade with an investor, then he wants to get out of that position at a profit that compensates him for the risk of taking that position for the benefit of the counterparty in the first place. The concern here is not about the classic market-maker and his reasonable modus operandi. It's one thing to earn the spread as compensation for facilitating an investor's trade. But it's another thing altogether to earn the spread, or the rebate, for its own sake. Making a trade, say, buying on a rally with confidence you can soon sell it at a profit, with no other purpose than to earn a spread and/or rebate, just seems like a waste of market resources. To some, the practice at best sits on the cusp of silliness and at worst is an inexcusable misuse of a market.

Rogue Trading and Contagion

Beyond the host of concerns about intentional high-frequency trading—is it fair, does it increase volatility, and so on—there is also the nasty matter of unintentional trading. The U.S. equity supermarket is a system of systems of systems, each designed and constructed more or less independently by fallible human hands. As anyone with experience in HFT well knows, unintended or "bad trades" happen all the time. Many of these are the result of mistakes made during the design, building, or testing of an HFT system—the complexity of which can moisten the brow of even the most veteran software engineer. Moreover, some errors are the result of forces well outside the control of the HFT firm itself; for example, the availability of a crucial network link between its data center and an exchange, or a problem with the exchange system, itself a formidably complex assemblage of networked hardware and software. The list of all possible causes of bad trades would be a long one indeed.

In most cases, the damage from a bad trade is restricted to the HFT firm itself. On a recent Christmas Eve, one HFT firm (it's likely every HFT firm out there could tell a story or two like this) experienced a perfect storm of multiple computer failures—a bad tick in the market data feed, an improperly communicated code change, a bug that slipped through testing, two independent safety devices unintentionally disabled—any one of which would have been benign had it happened in isolation. But because they happened all at once, the system sprayed the market with hundreds of thousands of improperly priced orders. Enough of these were filled that Bad Santa took nearly half a million dollars from this unlucky firm in a matter of seconds. (Of course, while it ruined their employees' Christmas, the counterparties of those bad trades found quite unexpected gifts in their own stockings.)

The damage would have been far worse were it not for the so-called "obvious error rules" of the exchanges where the trades were made. Knowing that unintentional trades are bound to happen, most exchanges will consider busting the trade (i.e., wiping it from the books as if it never happened). Or they may adjust the price so the loss isn't quite so horrific to the party that screwed up. But not every bad trade is breakable or adjustable, and many times doing so requires the consent of the counterparty, which is a bit like asking a pit bull to relinquish the steak that fell out of a window and into its yard.

The risk of self-inflicted wounds such as those from the Bad Santa event, where damage was contained to the HFT firm itself, is not the real concern here. The greater risk is that an error will cost someone else money (say, by jamming the circuit into an exchange with a flood of meaningless orders such that others can't tell the exchange to cancel an order before the market moves against it) or so extend the obligations of the rogue trading party they risk defaulting on those obligations (say, by unintentionally committing to buy 50 million shares of some stock when they have only the capital to buy 1 million).

The larger firms said to be engaged in HFT no doubt have increasingly rigorous processes in place to ensure bad things like this don't happen. The problem, though, is that nearly any firm, no matter how inexperienced, can engage in HFT by paying for a service known as *direct market access*, or DMA. The idea here is that a large firm, say, a major brokerage, can lease to third parties its high-speed exchange connections and trading rights. Also known as *sponsored access*, or *naked access*, the lessor firm under current rules is not obligated to monitor the trading activity of the lessee in a way that would prevent it from sending potentially havoc-wreaking orders into the markets.

The unintended and deleterious interaction of the HFT strategies is more than theoretical. For example, one firm may have programmed its system such that it always wants to be alone on the bid or the offer. Another firm may have a program instructing its system to always join the market. Clearly, those programs can't both coexist for long. Could interactions such as these lead to something like a contagion, where one unintentional interaction leads to another, which leads to another, and so on? Imagine a bug that moves a market sharply downward (e.g., from a system programmed to sell instead of buy, on some obscure branch of program logic) that kicks off another firm's system to do the same (due to or exacerbated by its own bug), then another firm's, such that human panic takes over and now it's not just computers placing sell orders but people on telephones doing the same.

Now, as noted earlier, fundamental traders may get into the picture and slow or even stop the erroneous trend—and ultimately reverse it. But who can say for sure? Even after all HFT systems are turned off, the market could continue to spiral down due to plain old human panic. Granted, such a scenario is ultrasimplistic and disregards all sorts of safety mechanisms that could stop the contagion. Still, and unfortunately, each of those safety mechanisms is also the work of human hands and subject to its own unforeseen errors. Things that once seemed outrageously theoretical do have a habit of happening. Many of us remember Black Monday, the 1987 market crash widely attributed to unforeseen problems with what was then known as program trading.

Much more recently, high-frequency trading was certainly behind one of the most rapid sell-offs ever—followed by an equally rapid recovery—on March 6, 2010. That afternoon, investors watched dumbfounded as the Dow tumbled to a 9 percent loss in a matter of minutes. Then, with people wondering if it was 2008 all over again, the markets recovered most of the loss. No "flash crash" like that had ever happened before. As these words are written, investigation into the matter is just beginning. But it's entirely plausible that some HFT firm's trading engines reacted to a market event with excessive sell orders, which were taken as cues by other HFT engines to do the same, which in turn served to entice others to jump on the bandwagon. Indeed, it's hard to imagine anything other than rogue machines causing such a rapid and extreme disruption of the market. The computerized race to the bottom stopped only when some stocks reached a price of zero. Zero! Then, it appears other engines spotted what were outrageously good bargains and began snapping them up with a flood of buy orders, starting yet another bandwagon effect, this time in an upward direction. It may turn out that HFT did not start the decline, but may have at the least poured oil onto an already slippery slope.

Just as nobody can guarantee an airplane will make it safely to its destination, nobody can be completely sure there won't be contagious and system-wide errors from time to time. We could, however, borrow from the aviation industry and its National Transportation Safety Board and take reasonable and proactive measures to learn from incidents, as we do with air disasters. Imagine a body of investigators charged with studying each and every glitch until its cause is well understood, then recommending preventative measures to be applied to all HFT systems. We don't have something like a Securities Trading Safety Board, but perhaps we should.

Colocation

An HFT firm with its servers colocated in NASDAQ's data center in Carteret, New Jersey, will get its orders into the NASDAQ matching engine roughly 500 microseconds before a firm located somewhere else in the tristate region can, and something like 15 milliseconds before a firm way off in Chicago possibly could. If the firm's servers are similarly located in Secaucus and Weehawken, they will also beat the competition into most of the other stock and options exchanges. Is such a firm at an unfair advantage to everyone else? Plenty of people seem to think so.

The once arcane term *colocation*, used only by industry insiders and only the most geekish of those folks, referring to the placement of HFT servers in the same data centers as the exchange-matching engines, turned into quite a hot button in 2009. The advantage of the colocated firm relative to the noncolocated firm is beyond question. But is it unfair? If colocation space is available to anyone willing to pay for it, it's hard to see the unfairness of it. Multiple sell-side HFT firms certainly take advantage of colocation, and there's nothing stopping buy-side firms from doing the same.

If colocation were deemed unfair, could not the same argument be made regarding the networking and computing hardware some trading firms choose to buy? Or the human talent—the rock star quantitative analysts, traders, and developers—some firms choose to hire? One can shell out millions just on network routers and switches, and tens of millions for the best of the best people. It may turn out that the concern over colocation per se withers over time, unless it turns out, of course, that some firms do indeed have access to colocation for unfair reasons, say, bribery or what have you. Then it's a fair complaint indeed.

OVER THE LINE?

When it comes to the trading of securities, the lines between legal versus illegal, compliant versus noncompliant, and good-for-firms versus good-for-investors seem forever razor-thin. And gray. The rule book governing what you can and cannot do in the markets surely rivals IRS tax code in heft and, occasionally, ambiguity. As such, it requires no extraordinary leap of imagination to envision cream-of-the-crop legal counsel employed not only to ensure their clients are in compliance with the rules, but to find the loopholes in that book, the gray areas, and even perhaps identify those rules for which violation is so unlikely to be detected—or for which a court case is likely to go their way in the event they are caught—as to deem them ignorable. You might call it, as some do in the business, the dark side of high-frequency trading.

Floor Mannequins and Spacebar Traders

A cute example of dubious rule-stretching, from the early days of HFT, involves the "traders" that at least one firm was known to have placed on the floor of a securities exchange where electronic quoting was permitted only by firms with traders physically in the crowd.[4] The firm contracted with a temp agency to provide men and women, with little or no trading experience, who the firm directed to simply stand in the trading pit beside real traders and neither say nor do a thing. Like mannequins.[5] Meanwhile, their temporary employer streamed quotes and orders into the exchange electronically and made quite a lot of money.

Around the same time the mannequin traders were getting an up-close if uncomfortable view of a trading floor, some exchanges banned the electronic generation and submission of trade orders (as by an electronic eye or take-out engines, scanning a market for mispriced securities). Crafty HFT firms are said to have modified their electronic eyes to detect a trading opportunity automatically but to wait for a

---

[4] Those rules have since been lifted.

[5] The practice apparently led to some dicey interactions along these lines. Trader: "What's your market?" Mannequin: "What?" Trader: "I said what's your freaking market?" Mannequin: "I don't know." Trader: "What do you mean you don't know?" Mannequin: "I don't know what you're talking about." Trader: "Why are you here?!" Mannequin: "I need to go to the bathroom."

human to press a spacebar before sending the order to the exchange. These firms would then have relatively low-paid administrative assistants rotate in and out of the mind-numbing (and no doubt humiliating) duty of sitting at a computer for long stretches of time, quickly pressing the spacebar over and over, as quickly as they could, while reading a book or magazine or chatting with passersby. These bans against electronic order entry have since been lifted and, with them, presumably, the need for spacebar traders.

HFT firms take extraordinary measures to keep their operations secret. The mere length and density of typical employee nondisclosure agreements are enough to keep any employee's mouth shut, even after the employee leaves the firm, when she may be prevented even from cooperating with law enforcement until first notifying the former employer. The mere intensity of such measures begs a natural question: Are the protections really in place to guard legitimate trade secrets, like formulas for new painkillers or soft drinks? Or is their real purpose to hide questionable activity going on behind tightly locked doors? And here's another concern: It's human nature, at least for some humans, when they know nobody is looking, to do things they might otherwise not. Would some HFT practices even happen if the persons responsible knew they might one day have to explain themselves? Granted, when the rules of any game are unclear, you can't blame a player for taking the benefit of the doubt. But what's too far? Are some of the practices of the more aggressive and well-heeled HFT firms just savvy trading? Or cheating? Let's look at a couple more.

Front-Running Flash Orders

By the time you read this, flash orders may have been banned in U.S. markets and relegated to a footnote in the history of

Wall Street. For many, the flash order controversy of 2009 indeed defined high-frequency trading; had flash orders never come to be, it's likely the HFT controversy would never have even erupted. It's easy to appreciate how they sparked the controversy. To the casual reader of the news, flash order trading seemed like front-running, plain and simple. An HFT firm paid a fee to an exchange in return for an early look at a customer order, allowing the firm to get in front of it. There is a grain or two of truth in there, but not much more.

The original intent of flash ordering was undeniably benign and even, at first blush, beneficial to the public investor. They were invented primarily in response to requirements on exchanges (and ATSs) imposed by Regulation NMS, which stipulated that an exchange was not allowed to fill a customer order if the customer could get a better price on another exchange or ATS. In other words, if the exchange was not on the NBBO, it could not fill the order and was generally required to "send the order away" to an exchange with the better price. To violate this rule and fill such a customer order is known as "trading through" the NBBO. The exchange was permitted, however, to inform its liquidity providers of the order before sending it away—by exposing, or "flashing," it to them for a brief time, on the order of 20 or 30 microseconds[6]—ostensibly to see if any of them wished to improve their price to the NBBO. That all sounds good, right?

The problem is that recipients of the flash orders could conceivably use the information not to improve their bid or offer but to get in front of that customer order. For example,

---

[6] Not every place calls these things "flash" orders. Direct Edge, for example, calls them IOI (indication of interest) orders, which they send to their ELPs (Extended Liquidity Providers) or "dark pools," but only when the customer order is indicated as ELP-eligible. Indeed, Direct Edge defends this practice in part by pointing out that customers can opt out of flashing.

if a flash order recipient knew that a customer wanted to buy, when the local exchange had a best offer of $1.10 and another exchange had a best offer of $1.09, the recipient of that information could quickly go out and buy up all the shares offered at $1.09, then immediately sell them locally to the customer at $1.10—since that was now the NBBO, due to the lightning-speed trade of the $1.09—and make a quick little profit of a penny. The exchange might also resort to flashing even when it is on the NBBO but for not enough size to fill the order. Continuing the example, perhaps the local exchange has 200 shares offered at $1.09 but the customer wants to buy 600 shares. The locals are flashed, and the unscrupulous recipient buys up the 200 offered locally in addition to any offered at that price on an away exchange.

There is another beneficiary to the flash order front-runner. This is the internalizer, a broker/dealer (BD) who takes the other side of his customer orders. He is allowed to do so under certain conditions, chief among them being that he trade with his customer at the NBBO. Were a BD in this scenario to internalize a customer buy order right after the action of the front-running flash order recipient, he could do so at $1.10 rather than the now-eradicated NBBO of $1.09.

The problem with this theory is that it may be just that—theory. As these words are written, there is as yet no convincing pile of evidence that any recipient of flash orders actually abused them in this way. Some defenders of the practice point out the comparatively small sizes of orders that tend to be flashed and the small amount of money to be made by getting in front them, implying that it just wouldn't be worth the trouble of an HFT firm to risk a front-running charge, no matter how flimsy. Of course, there may actually be evidence of flash order front-running out there. And when and if it surfaces, someone will have quite a lot of explaining to do.

Among the most vocal defenders of flash orders are some of the options exchanges, due to subtle but meaningful differences between the options markets and stock markets. In stock markets, fees for taking liquidity (the "take" fee of a maker-taker exchange) are capped. In the options markets they currently are not. (This may change.) And at some options exchanges, such as the CBOE and ISE, customers are not charged transaction fees. If you are one of these exchanges, then, and receive a customer order when you are not on the NBBO, sending the order away requires you to foot the cost of doing so (i.e., paying the take fee and transmission costs). This cuts into your profits, of course, so you would very much like the option (so to speak) of flashing those orders to liquidity providers.[7]

Fake Customer Trading

Some options exchanges such as the CBOE and ISE are considered "customer priority" exchanges in that orders received from supposedly nonprofessional trading firms—also known as customer or retail orders—have two significant advantages over orders from professional firms. First, they pay no fee to the exchange. Second, if they are on a market alongside noncustomer firms (e.g., market-makers), they are filled first. For example, if an exchange is a one dollar bid for 500 with 300 representing customer interest and 200 market-maker interest, a market order to sell 300 would

---

[7] At the CBOE, flash orders are known as HAL orders, for Hybrid Agency Liaison. There are other types of uses of HAL beyond flashing potential NBBO trade-throughs. The CBOE has no love for flash orders and uses them only because it feels it has no choice. If it had its druthers, broker/dealers would never send flashable orders in the first place. Stock exchanges are less inclined to take this stand, because, unlike options exchanges such as the CBOE, they generally earn a fee even for customer trades.

be filled entirely by the customers on the bid. The market-makers have to wait. Trading as a nonprofessional thus has substantial advantages. And as you can imagine, some very professional trading firms have apparently found a way to get them for themselves.

Consider the large trading firm consisting of multiple, legally distinct entities. One of these entities might be registered as a broker-dealer, or market-maker, or some other designation such that any orders it submits are considered professional trade orders by the receiving exchange. This firm might have developed an amazingly impressive HFT system but finds itself losing orders to customers who happen to be alongside them on markets. With not too much difficulty, such a multientity firm could submit orders from one of its entities not registered as a professional.

Using the very same system developed for the pros—the quantitative analytics and algorithms, the bleeding-edge software, the high-speed networks, and everything else—these orders could be routed through a broker-dealer (even one owned, say, by the same conglomerated trading firm, thus hiding things even more) and thus arrive at the CBOE or ISE as anonymous "customer" orders. They are filled ahead of the professional orders—and ahead of real customer orders if the firm can get them in more quickly, which is rather to be expected given its technological superiority—and not be charged transaction fees, to boot. Even better, on exchanges where there are significant costs to being a legitimate market-maker, the faux customers can post two-sided markets just like a market-maker can, in order to receive market order allocations and whatnot, without going through the hassle and expense of being a real market-maker. The practice is alarming for its chutzpah and would be laughable were it not for real customers having to compete with the fakes, all to jump ahead in line and get a break on trading fees. It's not entirely unlike a billionaire being driven to a soup kitchen, then sending in his dressed-down chauffer to fetch him a free plate of food.

Fake customer trading like this stymied the affected options exchanges for years, which naturally would have preferred to receive fees from these so-called customers. The exchanges received some relief in late 2008 and 2009, when the SEC permitted them to treat some of these "customers" as professionals based on their trading patterns. It still leaves a loophole for the particularly crafty firm to get through (say, by spinning off a large number of fake trading firms such that no one of them trips the limit), but it's something.

TO BE EXPECTED?

Given the mind-numbing complexity of high-frequency trading, not to mention the forever shifting market structures, the newness of it all, and—oh yes—the great deal of money to be made, it's no surprise there are plenty of opportunities for getting away with dubious practices. And firms only too happy to seize them. Fortunately, many of the smash-and-grab practices are by nature self-eliminating, working only until the rules change and/or others catch on to the jig.[8] This doesn't

---

[8] It reminds me of the old joke about counterfeiters who for many years supposedly got away with using fake bills with odd denominations—seven-dollar bills, thirteen-dollar bills, and such—on unsophisticated merchants in the frontier days of the western United States. One day, after this had been going on for some time, a counterfeiter rode into town and asked a grocer if he could break an eighteen-dollar bill. "Sure can," said the grocer obligingly. "Would you like three sixes or two nines?"

mean, of course, that regulators and law enforcement and public investors should ignore the practices. To the contrary, with the growing scope and scale and interconnectedness of the markets—not to mention the vast amount of investor capital at risk—it makes more sense than ever to shine some light into the dark side of high-frequency trading.

NOW WHAT?

As these words are written in 2010, scrutiny of high-frequency trading continues slowly but surely—too slowly for its detractors and too surely for its defenders. The only thing everyone seems to agree on is that it's happening. And it's happening huge. In the time it takes to cablecast an HFT debate (smackdown is a more apt description for some of them) on CNBC, hundreds of computer servers humming away in New Jersey move billions of bits of data on and off the data highways connecting U.S. exchanges, making an equal number of decisions ultimately affecting the investment account balances of virtually every family in America. We can only hope they get it right.

The Securities and Exchange Commission has its crosshairs on several aspects of HFT. It has proposed a ban on flash orders and naked access. It wants to shine light onto dark pools by doing things like forcing them to display more of their order books and by including more detailed information about trade executions once they are made.[1] The SEC currently seeks public comment on high-frequency trading, colocation, and overall fairness of the markets; it should get an earful.

---

[1] Today, and amazingly to some given their growing dominance of the U.S. stock market, dark pools report their trades more-or-less anonymously as generic "off-floor" trades. The SEC is decidedly understated when it proposes to "amend existing rules to require real-time disclosure of the identity of the dark pool that executed the trade." [*SEC Issues Proposals to Shed Greater Light on Dark Pools*, http://www.sec.gov/news/press/2009/2009-223.htm.]

Plenty of folks would prefer that the free markets take care of policing high-frequency trading; if there is money to be made from it, innovative firms may do just that. But you don't have to dig too deeply into Wall Street history to see that a great many of the commonsense rules against egregious market practices were written not by the invisible hand of the free market but by the strong arm of Uncle Sam.

What do the high-frequency traders themselves think of the clamor? They're not saying much. The established ones may be too busy keeping ahead of the newcomers—the "gold in them thar hills" effect—by moving beyond the practically quaint capabilities of mere high-frequency trading. They speak now of *ultra* high-frequency (or UHF) trading, so the extent to which things will only speed up is anyone's guess.

For the time being, we'll just need to wait and see how well the SEC fares in its proposed reforms and how well the HFT firms fare at fighting them off. We'll continue to hear defenders of HFT remind everyone there is nothing to fear, that all of this is a perfectly natural evolution of the markets and ultimately beneficial to everyone. And from others, we'll hear how much of a scam the whole HFT thing is, that Wall Street has once again been infested by sharks, only this time the sharks have Ph.D.s in math and computer science. The truth can no doubt be found where it usually is in such debates, somewhere right in the middle. Yes, we'll no doubt learn, some people are using new technology to get away with questionable practices that need to be ended—but not everyone is. And yes, HFT is as evolutionary as the internal combustion engine—but it does introduce all-new risks to fairness and safety, risks we ignore at our own peril.

---

active trading: The placing of a trade order in an attempt to interact with a displayed bid or offer, i.e., to hit the bid or lift the offer. The opposite of passive trading.

algorithm: A set of repeatable instructions for the completion of some task, such as the trading of securities.

algorithmic trading: The computerized placing of trade orders, typically by a buy-side party, in accordance with specific instructions and objectives embodied in a software program. *See also* black-box trading *and* robo trading.

alpha: The difference between a security's actual market price and the theoretically correct price. Used heavily by statistical arbitrageurs to identify so-called "mispriced" securities.

API (application programming interface): Generally, the software interface between programs. In HFT, refers to the software interface of an exchange-matching engine or market data publisher.

arbitrage: The simultaneous buying of a security at one price and selling it (or an equivalent security or portfolio) at another, higher price in order to earn a risk-free profit.

arbitrageur: One who practices arbitrage.

ask: The price at which some party is willing to sell some number of securities. Also known as offer.

ATS (alternative trading system): An SEC-approved forum for the trading of securities outside a traditional exchange.

at-the-money option: A call or put option whose strike price is equal to that of the current market price of the underlying security. Exercising such an option results in no payoff to the option buyer.

bad trade: An unintentional, money-losing trade, e.g., the purchase of a security for more than it is worth. *See also* pick off.

bandwidth: In networking, a measure of the "size" of a circuit, or how many bytes of data can be moved over a given period of time; roughly analogous to the diameter of a garden hose.

basis point: One one-hundredth of a percent. 6 basis points = .06 percent, 150 basis points = 1.5 percent, and so on.

basket: The set of stocks underlying an index; for example, the 500 stocks from which the S&P 500 index gets its value.

BATS: Stock exchange and options exchange with matching engines currently (March 2010) housed in Weehawken, NJ.

BBO (best bid and offer): The highest bid price and lowest offer price, and associated quantities available at those prices, at a given exchange or displayed ATS at a given time.

beta: From the capital asset pricing model, the ratio of an individual stock's price or return relative to that of the market overall or an index of which the stock is a component. Provides a measure of a stock's sensitivity to changes in the index.

bid: The price at which some party is willing to buy some number of securities.

binomial: A method of pricing an option involving the use of a multistage lattice (tree) of possible price changes for the underlier, whereby the price can change to one of only two possible prices at each branch. *See also* trinomial.

black-box trading: *See* algorithmic trading.

Black-Scholes: Typically refers to both the Nobel-winning formula for pricing options and to the partial differential equation from which the formula is derived.

block order: An order to trade a relatively large number of securities, large enough to potentially move the market away from the party placing the order.

BOX (Boston Options Exchange): An options exchange with matching engines currently (March 2010) housed in Newark, NJ, but scheduled to move to Secaucus, NJ.

broker-dealer (BD): Generally, the intermediary between a customer who wants to trade and the exchange where the trade is ultimately done.

bug: An unintended and undesirable behavior of a computer system.

buy-side: Refers loosely to institutional investors and others who wish to hold securities for the inherent benefit of doing so, and generally take liquidity from providers. *See also* sell-side.

C++: Programming language of choice for many HFT system developers.

C2: Price-time options exchange planned by the CBOE, with matching engine to be located in Secaucus, NJ.

call option: A derivative security that grants its buyer the right, but not the obligation, to buy an underlying security at a specified strike price on or before a specified expiration date.

carry: The difference between a futures contract delivery price and the current price of the underlying security or commodity, resulting from the cost (or benefit) of delaying the purchase/sale. Includes interest, expected dividends, and other factors depending on the underlier.

CBOE (Chicago Board Options Exchange): A customer-priority, specialist-style options exchange with matching engines in the Chicago Loop.

CFTC (Commodity Futures Trading Commission): U.S. regulatory body overseeing CME, ICE, and other futures exchanges. Plays a very similar role as the SEC.

clearing: The process kicked off after a trade order fill that validates counterparties, verifies the accuracy of the trade, and ultimately results in an exchange of funds.

CME (Chicago Mercantile Exchange): Futures exchange with matching engines in Chicago.

code: The human-readable computer instructions written in a programming language such as C++, which is compiled into executable software programs.

colocation: The practice of placing HFT system servers in the same data center as an exchange-matching engine to minimize the latency of communicating with the exchange for market data and order/quote submission.

compliance: The running of a trading operation in keeping with applicable laws and regulations.

counterparty: One of the two parties to a trade.

CPU (central processing unit): *See* processor.

CQS (Consolidated Quotation System): *See* CTA.

cross-connect: The allowance of two servers in a colocation facility to interact with one another at very high bandwidth without going through an outside network connection, such as between an HFT firm's electronic eye and the matching engine of an exchange.

crossed market: A situation in which the bid price at one exchange or ATS is greater than the offer price at another exchange or ATS. *See also* locked market.

CTA (Consolidated Tape Association): Market data feed that includes real-time updates of quotes (CQS) and trades (CTS) from across all stock exchanges. Owned and operated by NYSE and originates from Weehawken, NJ (scheduled to move to Mahwah, NJ).

CTS (Consolidated Tape System): *See* CTA.

customer priority: A protocol for filling orders whereby those orders originating from nonprofessional traders are filled first. *See also* price-time priority.

dark pool: An ATS whose order book is not displayed.

delivery date: For a futures contract, the date on which the long party must buy the underlying commodity or security from the short party.

delivery price: For a futures contract, the agreed-upon price between buyer and seller of the underlying security, set when the contract is traded.

delta: One of the Greeks. Quantifies the sensitivity of an option price to changes in the underlying security price.

depth: A relative indication of how many securities are available to trade at BBO prices and other inferior prices.

derivative: A security, such as an option or futures contract, whose value is based primarily on that of some underlying security or commodity.

Direct Edge: Former ECN that became a stock exchange in March 2010.

display: To expose an order book to public access. Exchanges and ECNs display their order books. Dark pools, by definition, do not.

dividend: Periodic monetary distribution made by some publicly traded companies. Announced changes to dividends increase or decrease a stock's value.

DMA (direct market access): Controversial practice whereby broker-dealers and other firms with direct access to matching engines allow access to third parties. Also known as naked access.

ECN (electronic communication network): A type of ATS that facilitates the trading of securities much like an exchange does.

edge: Generally, the difference between trade price and theoretical price of a security.

electronic eye: A component of an HFT system that does active trading by sending IOC orders to desirable bids and offers.

elephant: Refers informally to one who places a very large order with substantial potential for moving the market.

E-mini: One of several electronically traded (hence "E") equity index futures contracts traded at the CME. Often refers specifically to the highly liquid E-mini S&P futures (ES) contract.

equity: Another name for stock.

ETF (exchange-traded fund): A listed security whose price reflects the current price of an index and trades very much like a stock. Also known as an index tracking stock.

event: Something that happens that is likely to affect the price of a stock.

exchange: In the United States, a regulated marketplace for the public trading of financial securities.

expiration: For an option, the last date at which the buyer of an option may exercise his or her right to buy (in the case of a call option) or sell (in the case of a put option) the underlying security.

extensibility: A desirable feature of any software system that facilitates the future modification of the system or addition of new capabilities.

extranet: A private computer network wherein subscribers typically pay for access to a set of certain computers on the network.

fair market value: *See* theoretical value.

FDM (finite difference method): A procedure for calculating the price of an option using a discrete set of steps or lattice. Closely related to the trinomial method, but with multiple root nodes as compared to the single root node of a trinomial.

fill: The successful completion of a trade order by an exchange, and notification of the party submitting the order they have bought or sold securities in accordance with the terms of their order. *See also* print.

finite difference method: *See* FDM.

FIX (Financial Information eXchange protocol): An industry-standard messaging format and interface software for receiving market data, submitting orders, listening for responses, etc.

flash order: An indication to certain parties associated with an exchange, in advance of public dissemination, of a customer's desire to trade at a price inferior to those at the current exchange. Intended to facilitate the stepping up of prices by flash order recipients. Controversial due to concern it can actually facilitate front-running.

forward interest: The interest on a hypothetical loan starting at some point in the future. *See also* spot interest.

front-running: An illegal attempt to profit using advanced, private knowledge of someone else's trade by trading before they do.

futures contract: A derivative security that obligates the long party to buy (and the short party to sell) an underlying commodity or security at a specified price on a certain future date.

gamma: One of the Greeks. Quantifies the sensitivity of an option's delta to changes in the underlying security price.

Greek: Informal but widely used name given to one of several standard, quantifiable measures of an option price's sensitivity to one of the factors affecting its price. The most common Greeks are delta, gamma, vega, theta, and rho.

GUI (graphical user interface): Software program that facilitates human interaction with a computer or system.

hedge: A trade intended to offset future changes to the value of some existing security or portfolio. Used extensively by options market-makers to help lock in a profit margin.

hidden-size order: *See* iceberg order.

historical volatility: Volatility as calculated using historical prices. *See* volatility.

hitting a bid: To submit a trade order to sell at a currently displayed bid price.

ICE (Intercontinental Exchange): Futures exchange with matching engines in Chicago.

iceberg order: A size order revealed to an exchange in small pieces in order to minimize the market impact of the order.

implied volatility (IV): Volatility backed out of an option pricing model using market prices. Indicates the current volatility presumed by the market.

improve (a market): To place a bid higher than the current best bid, or an offer less than the current best offer.

index: An average price of a basket of securities; for example, S&P 500, NASDAQ 100, Russell 2000.

institutional investor: A buy-side firm or trader responsible for a large portfolio, such as for a mutual fund or pension fund. Tends to place relatively large orders.

internalize: The filling of a broker-dealer customer's trade order by the broker-dealer itself. Trade price must be on the NBBO and fulfill other requirements.

in-the-money option: A call (put) option whose strike price is less than (greater than) that of the current market price of the underlying security. Exercising such an option results in a payoff to the option buyer.

inventory: The current net positions of, typically, a market-maker. When an inventory contains relatively large exposures in certain securities, the market-maker can lean her bids and/or offers in those securities in an attempt to reduce those exposures.

IOC (immediate-or-cancel) order: A type of order whereby the exchange attempts to fill as much of the order size as it can, then automatically cancels any remaining quantity. Controversial for its potential use for aggressively detecting hidden liquidity.

IOI (indication of interest): Similar to a flash order, used by an exchange to alert certain parties, such as dark pools, of an order.

ISE (International Securities Exchange): A customer-priority, specialist-style options exchange with matching engines in Secaucus, NJ.

join (a market): To place a bid whose price equals that of the current best bid or an offer that equals the current best offer.

latency: The time it takes for some task to be completed on a computer system or for data to travel from one point to another.

leg: One of the single-contract option components of a spread. Most spreads (e.g., straddles, strangles) have two legs. Some have three (e.g., butterfly) and some have four (e.g., condor).

legal width: The maximum spread allowed on certain exchanges.

LIBOR (London Interbank Offered Rate): An interest rate widely used as a risk-free interest rate when pricing options and other derivative securities.

lifting an offer: To submit a trade order to buy at a currently displayed offer price.

limit order: An order to buy or sell a security at a specified price. *See also* market order.

linkage: The system by which U.S. exchanges are connected with one another for the primary purpose of complying with NBBO trade price restrictions. For example, an exchange receiving a customer order when it is not on the NBBO can use linkage to "route the order away" to an exchange that is.

Linux: An open-source computer operating system favored by many high-frequency trading firms for its overall efficiency and relative ease of customization and optimization.

liquidity: A measure of the relative ability of potential traders to find counterparties, as indicated by the market spread and depth. More liquid markets have more trading activity than less liquid markets.

load balancing: The important HFT system design and implementation function whereby work is spread out evenly among software components and/or servers in order to minimize bottlenecks and thus facilitate the greatest possible throughput.

locate: To borrow shares for the facilitation of selling them short.

locked market: A situation in which the bid price at one exchange or ATS is equal to the offer price at another exchange or ATS. *See also* crossed market.

long position: A position resulting from the net buying of a security whose value increases as does the market price of the security.

loose coupling: A desirable feature of a software system in which components are highly independent of one another, performing work behind strictly defined interfaces, such that changes to one component are relatively less likely to in turn negatively affect the operation of another.

lot: In a trade order, the quantity of securities to be traded. For example, a one-lot is for one security, a ten-lot is for ten, and so on.

low latency: The desirable feature of a high-frequency trading system whereby computational and transmission latencies are minimized as much as possible in order to gain advantages over other high-frequency trading firms.

maker-taker: A pricing policy of some exchanges where active traders pay a fee, some of which is distributed to the associated passive trader.

margin: Funds posted up front by traders or trading firms to ensure their ability to meet their trading obligations.

market-maker: A trader or firm that uses passive trading to express willingness to buy and/or sell a given security at specified bid and offer prices, respectively. Also known as a specialist.

market order: An order to buy at the current market offer or sell at the current market bid. *See also* limit order.

matching engine: The electronic point of entry to the order book of an exchange and the recipient of incoming quotes and trade orders. Located primarily in data centers in New Jersey and Illinois, where HFT firms can colocate their servers to minimize the latency of exchange interactions.

microprice: The calculated price of a stock for high-frequency trading purposes.

microsecond: One millionth of a second.

midprice: The midpoint between a bid and offer price.

millisecond: One thousandth of a second.

naked access: *See* DMA.

naked short: The short selling of stock without borrowing it first. Highly risky.

nanosecond: One billionth of a second.

NASDAQ: Stock exchange with matching engines in Carteret, NJ.

NASDAQ 100: Popular index based on 100 stocks listed on the NASDAQ exchange.

NASDAQ NOM (NASDAQ Options Market): Price-time priority options exchange with matching engines in Carteret, NJ.

NASDAQ PHLX (NASDAQ PHLX Market): Customer-priority, specialist-style options exchange with matching engines in Carteret, NJ.

NBBO (national best bid and offer): The net BBO across all U.S. exchanges and displayed ATSs at some point in time. *See also* BBO.

NYSE: Stock exchange with matching engines in Weehawken, NJ (scheduled to move to Mahwah, NJ).

NYSE Amex Options: Customer-priority, specialist-style options exchange with matching engines in Weehawken, NJ (scheduled to move to Mahwah, NJ).

NYSE Arca Options: Price-time priority options exchange with matching engines in Weehawken, NJ (scheduled to move to Mahwah, NJ).

OCC (Options Clearing Corporation): Clearing and settlement organization owned jointly by the U.S. options exchanges.

offer: The price at which some party is willing to sell some number of securities. Also known as ask.

OPRA (Options Price Reporting Authority): A consortium owned by the U.S. options exchanges charged with real-time dissemination of options market quotes and trade prices. Also refers to the market data feed. Analogous to CTA in the stock markets.

option: A derivative security whereby the buyer has the right but not the obligation to buy (if a call option) or sell (if a put option) an underlying security at a specified strike price on or before a specified expiration date. Used for both hedging and speculation.

order book: The current collection of unmatched bids and offers, and associated sizes, at an exchange or ATS. Exchanges and ECNs display their order books, whereas dark pools do not.

OTC (over the counter): A market for the private negotiation and execution of trades.

out-of-the-money option: A call (put) option whose strike price is greater than (less than) that of the current market price of the underlying security. Exercising such an option results in no payoff to the option buyer.

P&L (profit and loss): A measure of the economic effect of trading over some period of time; generally calculated by taking the difference between end-of-period market values of a portfolio and beginning-of-period values and subtracting costs incurred over the period.

pairs trade: A type of predictive trading strategy whereby two securities are identified whose price changes tend to follow each other's, allowing the trader to potentially trade in advance of a change in the price of the lagging security.

parallel processing: A computational technique whereby a single task is distributed across two or more processors, or cores of a single processor, which process parts of the task simultaneously in order to reduce the time required for completion of the overall task.

passive trading: The attempt to trade by the posting of a bid less than the current best offer, or an offer greater than the current best bid, in hopes someone else will hit your bid or lift your offer. Opposite of active trading.

penny jump: A strategy whereby a trader is motivated to improve his or her market in response to a relatively large market joiner.

PFOF (payment for order flow): Remuneration provided to a broker-dealer by a market-maker (or at the direction of a market-maker) as compensation for directing orders to the market-maker.

pick off: To force a bad trade onto another party, e.g., by hitting their bid or lifting their offer before they have a chance to modify it following a market event that changes the value of the security, or by interacting with their unintended and erroneous bid or offer.

pit: The physical place where human floor traders trade.

position: The number of shares, contracts, or other measure of securities resulting from trading those securities.

price-time priority: A protocol for filling orders whereby orders are filled in the order in which they are received. *See also* customer priority.

print: The public announcement of a trade. *See also* fill.

processor: The component of a computer where general-purpose computation takes place. *See also* CPU.

put option: A derivative security that grants its buyer the right, but not the obligation, to sell an underlying security at a specified strike price on or before a specified expiration date.

QA (quality assurance): The testing of a computer system to verify it works as intended and is sufficiently free of bugs to be put into use.

QQQQ: Highly liquid ETF that tracks the NASDAQ-1000 index. Known as "the Qs."

quant: A quantitative analyst or trader who formulates or implements trading strategies based on statistical or other mathematical principles.

quote: (n.) A bid and/or offer with associated sizes. (v.) To submit a bid and/or offer with associated sizes to an exchange or ATS.

rebate: Remuneration of a liquidity provider by an exchange. In very tight markets, may be the only source of payment to a market-maker, as when he buys and sells at the same price.

Regulation NMS: Influential regulation requiring, among other things, that trades be filled at no worse than the NBBO regardless of the exchange to which they are sent.

reserve order: An order held by an exchange for matching purposes, but not displayed.

resting order: A nonmarketable order on the book, i.e., an order to buy for a price less than or equal to the current best bid, or an order to sell at more than or equal to the current best offer.

rho: One of the Greeks. Quantifies the sensitivity of an option price to changes in the risk-free interest rate (typically LIBOR).

robo trading: *See* algorithmic trading.

round-trip: To buy at one price and sell at another, higher price; the daily grind of the market-maker and most high-frequency traders. *See also* scalp.

Russell 2000: Index of 2,000 stocks (the bottom 2,000 of the 3,000 largest stocks).

S&P 500: Index of 500 stocks, considered the bellwether for the U.S. stock market overall.

scalp: To buy at one price and sell at another, higher price; the daily grind of the market-maker and most high-frequency traders. *See also* round-trip.

scratch trade: A trade executed at a price equal to the theoretical value of the security. *See also* value trade.

SEC (Securities and Exchange Commission): U.S. regulatory body overseeing cash equity and option exchanges. Plays a very similar role as the CFTC.

sell-side: Refers loosely to market-makers, specialists, and high-frequency traders who provide liquidity to buy-side traders in return for a spread and/or exchange rebate.

server: A general-purpose computer, typically mounted in a rack in a data center and connected with other computers via a network.

SFTI (Secure Financial Transaction Infrastructure): A low-latency, fault-tolerant data network owned by NYSE and interconnecting most major exchanges.

short position: A position resulting from the net short selling of a stock, or writing of an option or shorting of a futures contract, whose value decreases as does the market price of the security.

short sale: The sale of a borrowed stock. Should the market price of the stock decline prior to returning the stock, the short seller makes a profit.

size: The number of shares or contracts associated with a given bid or offer, or trade order.

size order: *See* block order.

specialist: *See* market-maker.

Spider (SPDR): Highly liquid ETF based on the value of the S&P 500 index.

spot interest: The interest on a hypothetical loan starting now. *See also* forward interest.

spread: Typically refers to the difference between a bid and offer price. Also refers to an option trade consisting of multiple options combined to achieve a special payoff pattern.

SPX: The highly liquid cash-settled option on the S&P 500 stock index, traded exclusively at the CBOE. One of the few listed option contracts traded primarily by floor traders (as of March 2010).

statistical arbitrage: A trading technique by which trading and other data is heavily mined using statistical and other mathematical techniques in order to detect reliably predictable patterns.

stock: Everyone knows what stock is! ☺[1]

strategy: Another name for an option spread. Also refers to the standard techniques traders use to achieve trading profits.

strike price: The price at which the buyer of a call (or put) option has the right but not the obligation to buy (or sell) the underlying security.

---

[1] OK, a stock is a financial security, heavily traded in U.S. equity markets, representing some share of ownership of a company.

symbol: The abbreviated identifier of a stock, option, or futures contract.

synthetic: A synthetic option is a portfolio of securities intended to mimic the value of an actual option and is typically used by option market-makers to hedge their option positions. A synthetic futures position is a combination of long call option and short put option (or short call option and long put option) with the same strike and expiration, whose payoff mimics that of a futures contract on the same underlying security.

take out: To successfully hit a bid or lift an offer.

TCP/IP: The network protocol used by most networked computers to communicate with one another.

theoretical value: The calculated price of a given security, typically an option, such that neither counterparty to a trade at that price would experience an economic gain or loss. Also known as fair market value.

theta: One of the Greeks. Quantifies the sensitivity of an option price to changes in time remaining before expiration.

throughput: The measure of how much computation and/or data transfer is performed over some period of time. Analogous to the amount of water that comes out of a garden hose over some time.

tick: An expression used in different ways: (1) to refer to an indication of a price change from an exchange (change to bid price and/or size, offer price and/or size, or last trade price and/or size) (2) to refer to a change in price level (e.g., a stock "ticks up" to a new price) (3) to refer to the minimum increment by which a security's price can change (penny, nickel, etc.) or minimum price variation.

TOE (TCP/IP offload engine): An optional hardware device installed on a server for handling the moving of data on and off the network so the processor doesn't have to, freeing up the processor for other work.

trade-through: A trade that violates NBBO protection, i.e., an order to buy that is filled on some exchange at a price greater than the current best offer price on another exchange.

trinomial: A method of pricing an option involving the use of a multistage lattice (tree) of possible price changes for the underlier, where the price can change to one of two possible prices, or remain unchanged, at each branch. *See also* binomial *and* FDM.

TV: *See* theoretical value.

underlier: The security from which a derivative derives its value. For example, the underlier of a call option on Google stock is Google stock.

value trade: A trade executed at a price equal to the theoretical value of the security. *See also* scratch trade.

vega: One of the Greeks. Quantifies the sensitivity of an option price to changes in the volatility of the underlying security price.

volatility: A measure of the frequency and magnitude of changes to a stock price, typically given in terms of standard deviations. *See also* implied volatility *and* historical volatility.

volatility curve: A two-dimensional data construct mapping volatility levels to a range of strike prices or expiration dates. Can be visualized as an x-y graph with volatility levels on the y- or vertical axis, and strike prices or expiration dates on the x-axis.

volatility surface: A three-dimensional data construct combining both strike-based and expiration-based volatility curves into one construct, with strike prices on the x-axis, expiration dates on the y, and volatility levels on the z.

VPN (virtual private network): A set of computers connected by way of the public Internet but inaccessible to other computers.

VWAP (value-weighted average price): A securities price (typically a stock) based on the average of a sample of actual trade prices over some period of time.

WAN (wide area network): A set of geographically separated computers or networks of computers.

BIBLIOGRAPHY

Arnuk, Sal, and Joseph Saluzzi. "What Ails Us About High Frequency Trading?" *Advanced Trading Magazine* (September 30, 2009). Http://www.advancedtrading .com/algorithms/showArticle.jhtml?articleID= 220300593.

Co, Richard, and John W. Labuszewski. "Order Entry and Execution Methodologies." CME Group, Research & Product Development, 2009. White paper.

Donefer, Bernard S. "Algo's Gone Wild: Risk in the World of Automated Trading Strategies." 2009. Hft.thomson reuters.com.

Duhigg, Charles. "Stock Traders Find Speed Pays, in Milliseconds." *New York Times*, July 23, 2009. Http://www .nytimes.com/2009/07/24/business/24trading.html.

Esser, Angelika, and Burkart Monch. "The Navigation of an Iceberg: The Optimal Use of Hidden Orders." EFA 2005 Moscow Meetings Paper, January 26, 2005. Http://ssrn .com/abstract=654446.

"Goldman May Lose Millions From Ex-Worker's Code Theft." Bloomberg, July 7, 2009. Http://www.bloomberg.com/ apps/news?pid=20601109&sid=aKZP.X9ayMr4.

Harris, Larry. *Trading and Exchanges: Market Microstructure for Practitioners*. Oxford, England: Oxford University Press, 2002.

Hasbrouck, Joel. *Empirical Market Microstructure: The Institutions, Economics and Econometrics of Securities Trading*. Oxford, England: Oxford University Press, 2007.

Johnson, Fawn. "SEC Seeks 'Baseline Information' on High-Frequency Traders." *Wall Street Journal*, October 28, 2009. Http://online.wsj.com/article/SB125674133414013217 .html.

McEachern Gibbs, Cristina. "Breaking It Down: An Overview of High-Frequency Trading." *Advanced Trading Magazine* (October 1, 2009). Http://www.advancedtrading.com/algorithms/showArticle.jhtml?articleID=220300267.

McEachern Gibbs, Cristina. "How High-Frequency Trading Became So Controversial." *Advanced Trading Magazine* (October 1, 2009). Http://www.advancedtrading.com/algorithms/showArticle.jhtml?articleID=220300262.

McIntyre, Hal. "ECN and ATS . . . The Electronic Future." White Paper for Wall Street Technology Association. The Summit Group, 1999. (soforum.com/library/ecn_ats .shtml).

Narang, Rishi K. *Inside the Black Box: The Simple Truth About Quantitative Trading*. Hoboken, NJ: Wiley Finance, 2009.

Patterson, Scott, and Geoffrey Rogow. "What's Behind High-Frequency Trading." *Wall Street Journal*, August 1, 2009. Http://online.wsj.com/article/SB124908601669298293 .html.

Silver, David. "A Short History of Fast Times on Wall Street." *New York Times*, September 17, 2009. Http://www.ny times.com/2009/09/18/opinion/18silver.html.

Smith, Cameron. "How High Frequency Trading Benefits All Investors," Traders Magazine Online News, March 17, 2010. Http://www.tradersmagazine.com/news/high -frequency-trading-benefits-105365-1.html?pg=1.

Spicer, Jonathan, and Herbert Lash. "Who's Afraid of High-Frequency Trading?" Reuters, December 2, 2009.

Sussman, Adam. "TABB Group Pulls Back the High-Frequency Trading Curtain." *Advanced Trading Magazine* (October 7, 2009). Http://www.advancedtrading.com/algorithms/ showArticle.jhtml?articleID=220301041.

U.S. Securities and Exchange Commission. "Concept Release on Equity Market Structure," January 14, 2010. [Release No. 34-61358; File No. S7-02-10] http://www.sec.gov/rules/concept/2010/34-61358.pdf.

Weild, David, and Edward Kim. "A Wake-up Call for America." Grant Thornton, Capital Market Series, November 2009. Http://www.gt.com/staticfiles/GTCom/Public%20

companies%20and%20capital%20markets/gt_wakeup
call.pdf.
Wilmott, Paul. "Hurrying into the Next Panic?" *New York Times*,
July 28, 2009. Http://www.nytimes.com/2009/07/29/
opinion/29wilmott.html.
Woodbine Associates. "Spotlight on High Frequency Trading."
August 13, 2009. (woodbineassociates.com/Woodbine
_Opinions.html).
Zendrian, Alexandra. "Don't Be Afraid of the Dark Pools."
May 18, 2009. Http://www.forbes.com/2009/05/18/
dark-pools-trading-intelligent-investing-exchanges.html.

INDEX

Active trading, 28, 29, 58, 59
Adverse selection, 93
Algorithmic strategies, 49
Algorithmic traders, 41, 48–49
Algorithms, 106–8
All-or-none orders, 27
Alpha, 84
Alternative trading systems
    (ATSs), 18–19
American-style options, 99, 100
Application programming
    interface (API), 122–23
Arbitrage
    options, 77–79
    spread, 80–83
    volatility, 69, 79–80
Arbitrage pricing theory, 35
Arbitrage strategies, 71–83
Arbitrageurs, 35–37
Ask price, 20
ATSs (alternative trading systems),
    18–19
At-the-money options, 70, 100
Auto Hedger, 156–58
Automated trading, viii, 3, 49
Autoquoters, 29

"Bad trades," 181–83
Bandwidth, 126–27
Baskets, 36–37, 73–74
BBO (best bid and offer), 20–21
Bermuda-style options, 99
Best bid and offer (BBO), 20–21
Beta, 86
Bid price, 20
Binary search algorithm, 107
Black-box traders, 41, 49

Black-Scholes partial differential
    equation, 96
Block orders, 24, 46
Butterflies, 82
Buy versus build decision, 98–101
Buy vol, 101
Buy-side traders, 31, 45

Call options, 11, 70
Call spreads, 82
Cash-settled contracts, 12
Chicago Board Options Exchange
    (CBOE), 15, 16
Citadel Investment Group, 1–3
Closing trade, 30
COB (complex order book), 82
Coding, 108
Colocation, 16, 123–25, 185–86
Colocation sites, 132–35, 186
Complex order book (COB), 82
Compliance Manager, 142–43
Confidentiality agreements, 2
Connectivity, 125–28
Coupling, 102
Cross-connect network links, 124
Crossed market, 35–36
Customer trading, 41–42
Customer-priority pricing model,
    44–45
Customized HFT systems, 97–98

Dark pools, 19
Dashboard, 169–71
Database, 136
Debate about HFT, 173–96
    benefits of HFT, 173–76
    colocation, 185–86

Michael Durbin is a former professional bowler inducted into the Professional Bowlers Association Hall of Fame in 1984 but is not, alas, the author of this book, which is too bad because a few tips on avoiding gutter balls would have certainly livened things up. The Michael Durbin who did write this book is a sometimes author, adjunct professor, and financial systems development consultant who has spent the bulk of his career thus far managing the design and development of software systems for the pricing and trading of financial derivatives.

That work began on the MOATS[1] team at the old First Chicago Capital Markets, where he discovered his possession of the rare gene that makes one actually enjoy working with interest rate mathematics and fixed income derivatives, before moving down the street and up the Sears Tower to Bank of America's massive swaps desk, where he helped morph the giant and overly complicated IRP system into the giant and overly complicated Advantage system. In 2003, enticed by the prospect of branching into options and eating lunches catered by Wolfgang Puck,[2] his job moved a few blocks up Franklin Street to the Citadel Investment Group, where he managed projects that led to the creation of a high-

---

[1] Mother Of All Trading Systems, managed by the one-of-a-kind Kurt Phillips-Zabel.

[2] This is true. Three meals a day plus snacks any time, and a Häagen-Dazs ice cream sundae cart they would literally wheel to the desk of any employee unable to walk from overeating.

frequency options trading system reportedly poised to take over the world any day now.

In 2005, he moved his family to Chapel Hill, North Carolina, to direct the development of an automated options market-making and proprietary trading operation for the Blue Capital Group—managing developers, securing trading rights and colocation space, dealing with compliance, and so on—and to develop a taste for vinegar-based barbecue sauce. While hanging out in the mild and enviable climes of the Carolina Piedmont, he also had the great opportunity to teach derivatives as an adjunct professor at the business schools of both Duke University and the University of North Carolina at Chapel Hill, where only once or twice did he show up for class wearing the wrong shade of blue. Michael Durbin (the author, not the bowler) can be reached at michael.durbin@ mac.com.